FANTASTIC *Opera*

FANTASTIC
Opera

The Great
Operas
Illuminated

By

JOHN MARTINEZ

Text by

F. PAUL DRISCOLL

Harry N. Abrams, Inc.,
Publishers

ACKNOWLEDGMENTS

Thanks to the following individuals for their help in preparation of this book: Elizabeth Diggans, Mrs. Francis P. Driscoll, Mary Erina Driscoll, Louise T. Guinther, Brian Kellow, Curtis Redhead, and the Merchandising Department of the Metropolitan Opera Guild. Special thanks to Ruth Peltason, our imaginative and supportive editor, and to Margaret Martinez, whose enthusiasm for this project have made it a reality.

—J. M. and F. P. D.

ABOUT THE AUTHORS

The talented John Martinez is an artist, designer, and art director. He is a former Senior Vice President and Creative Director at the Dentsu Corporation of America. The recipient of awards and honors from many professional organizations, including the Society of Illustrators, the Art Directors Club, and *Print* magazine, John Martinez further expanded his audience with the publication of fine silkscreen posters, which established his reputation worldwide. His work is in the permanent collections of the Library of Congress and the Museum of Modern Art, New York, which honored him for best art direction in their broadcast advertising show of 1994. The vast body of work by John Martinez spans film, television, the internet, and such print media as newspapers, magazines, and record covers. Much of his work has featured opera. Done strictly for pleasure, these paintings and drawings are primarily gouache and pencil on paper and range in size from three by five inches to three by four feet. His small opera images were first brought to the public in a series of framed prints commissioned by the Metropolitan Opera Guild in 1991. John Martinez and his family live in New York City.

F. Paul Driscoll is a writer, lecturer, and interviewer. He is a contributor and picture editor at *Opera News,* the publication of New York's Metropolitan Opera Guild, and his articles also appear in *Chamber Music, Stagebill,* and *Musical America.* In addition to his writing, he is a stage director, specializing in light opera; credits include the Kennedy Center for the Performing Arts, Washington, D.C., The College Light Opera Co., Falmouth, Mass., and the Scarsdale Summer Music Theatre. F. Paul Driscoll has been featured in opera education programs presented by the Cooper Union for the Advancement of Science and Art and by the lecture series of the Metropolitan Opera Guild's Education Department.

Contents

INTRODUCTION

Conversations on the subject of opera are either very long or very short, attenuated by unreasoning, unlistening, unanswerable partisanship or abbreviated in the interest of maintaining the general peace. Opera has engaged the passions and the pocketbooks of polite society for almost four centuries, its development an unruly but lively progression from the salons of late Renaissance Italy to the CD ROMs of the twenty-first century. Generally defined as a musical drama for singers and instrumental accompaniment, this most broadly inclusive of the performing arts takes commoners as well as kings for its heroes, embraces comedy, tragedy, farce and melodrama and sings in every language with grandeur as well as tenderness. Opera can throb with stark calamity or shudder with wildly improbable grotesquery, stimulate the mind, tug the heart strings, or tickle the fancy.

What makes a good opera? Time will tell. More than once a new work scorched by critics and public has re-emerged from its own ashes as a classic; *Il barbiere di Siviglia*, *Carmen*, *La Traviata*, *Tannhäuser*, and *Madama Butterfly*, now admired repertory standards, were all once regarded as failures. Just as frequently, a piece admired as a new jewel of inspiration is discovered to be paste after a few seasons and put away forever. Fashions in music drama change with the inexorable unpredictability of hemlines; today's Grand Old Man of the Theatre was probably yesterday's rebel.

In today's operatic repertory, new pieces struggle for pride of place with masterworks from the eighteenth and nineteenth centuries. Operas that have survived the test of time through repeated revivals are now frequently reimagined by stage directors and designers in settings their composers would have trouble recognizing, be it a *Carmen* transferred to the time of the Spanish Civil War—an event which took place some sixty years after its premiere—a *Così fan tutte* that replaces the sea coast of

eighteenth-century Naples with the neon-lit interior of an American roadside diner, or a *La Traviata* in which Violetta Valéry dies of AIDS-related illness rather than tuberculosis. The décor and the costumes may be unfamiliar but what (usually) remains unchanged are the music and the words, the chief components of operatic excellence whatever the time, place, or theatre.

This is probably a convenient juncture at which to mention that there are some people who don't like opera. They find it silly. Such persons are to be pitied rather than censured, for they have missed the point entirely. Opera's chief virtue is its unreality; to be truly worthy of its salt, an opera *should* be fantastic, an imagi-

native and impassioned combination of music, poetry, and dramatic action that creates a new world of experience beyond what is "real." These are the same people who always find opera "too long." Some are operas are admittedly on the lengthy side, but when you're in heaven five hours fly by.

The scarcity of patronage, the fallibility of critics, the disparity between singers' salaries (high) and composers' fees (low), and the burden of living with genius (or in living with a genius, as the case may be) have all been constants in the history of opera but nevertheless the form survives.

Fantastic Opera is an unconventional look at an art still in the process of reinventing itself after more than four hundred years of opening nights. The illustrations are designs for imaginary productions, fantasias on plot and characters, using the operas themselves as themes. These are not narrative drawings, but pictorial responses to the stories of love, betrayal, failure, and triumph that form the world's opera repertory. The text is not a comprehensive opera history or digest of plots but an album of reminiscence, gossip, musical trivia, and background information on the operas and their composers. The limitations of space have, alas, winnowed our available repertory to only a few dozen titles out of the hundreds of works available for examination; the omission of a few favorite operas was regrettable but unavoidable. We have tried to strike a balance between what will satisfy the enthusiast and pique the interest of the uninitiated in order to provide—just as opera itself does—a little bit of something for everyone.

L'Incoronazione di Poppea

Opera in a Prologue & 3 Acts
by

Claudio Monteverdi

(1567–1643)
and others

Libretto: G. F. Busenello
Premiere: Venice; 1642–43

As in the case of many prima donnas, it is difficult to establish an exact date and place of birth for opera itself. The country was most certainly Italy and the time near the close of the sixteenth century. In the late 1570s, a group of musicians, scholars, and poets calling themselves the Camerata met regularly in Florence at the home of Count Giovanni de' Bardi to discuss the creation of a new art form which would fuse the expressive power of poetry with that of music. In the polyphonic (many-voiced) style of composition then popular, lines of text were often sung in counterpoint and words were "buried" in the texture of the music. Composer Vincenzo Galilei, the father of the astronomer Galileo, wrote of the Camerata's propositions in the 1581 monograph *The Dialogue between Old and New Music*, advocating the unaffected declamation of text by a soloist performing to a simple accompaniment.

Among the Florentines who produced dramatic works on this order was the dashing composer/singer Jacopo Peri, whose *Dafne* (1598), its music now unfortunately lost, is generally considered to be the first true opera. In fact, many early operas were commissioned by wealthy patrons to celebrate special occasions and have not survived. The oldest opera now in the active repertory is a great one, written for a private performance in Mantua in 1607: *La Favola d'Orfeo* by Claudio Monteverdi. Monteverdi's setting of the Greek legend of Orpheus broke fresh musical and dramatic ground with its lean but plangent vocal lines and imaginative orchestration.

Following the death of his patron the Duke of Mantua in 1612, Monteverdi moved to Venice, where as the *maestro di cappella* of St. Mark's he produced a succession of magnificent sacred works that established his European reputation. It was in the prosperous Venetian Republic that opera evolved from court entertainment to a commercial proposition, a process begun in 1637 when the first great public opera house, the Teatro San Cassiano, was opened there by the Tron family. By century's end, there were eight active opera theatres in Venice. In 1640 Monteverdi, then almost seventy-three years of age (and by this time a priest), returned to opera composition and triumphed. His 1608 Mantuan opera *Arianna* was revived in Venice and the premiere of a new work, *Il Ritorno d'Ulisse in Patria*, followed soon after at the San Cassiano. The spectacular *L'Incoronazione di Poppea* was Monteverdi's last opera; he died, rich in honors, less than a year after its premiere.

Poppea is the story of the sybaritic Roman Emperor Nero and his mistress, the ambitious courtesan Poppea, who use murder, banishment, and psychological intimidation to achieve their unholy desires. Nero is ruled by lust rather than reason, his lover a woman impervious to all but her own pleasure. Evil may triumph over good in *Poppea* but its two leading characters are scarcely admirable, drawn as they are with a master's perception of human moral frailty. Now regarded as a probable collaboration between Monteverdi and at least two other composers, *Poppea* still shines with the sympathy and musical intelligence of one of the lyric theatre's greatest artists.

L'Incoronazione di Poppea
Her enemies all dispatched, the courtesan Poppea is crowned as consort to the Roman Emperor.

L'incoronazione di Poppea

Opera in a Prologue & 3 Acts
by
Claudio Monteverdi

GIULIO CESARE

Opera in 3 Acts

by

GEORGE FRIDERIC HANDEL

(1685–1759)

Libretto: NICOLA FRANCESCO HAYM
Premiere: LONDON, KING'S THEATRE, HAYMARKET; FEBRUARY 20, 1724

Above:
Orlando (1733)

Opposite:
Giulio Cesare
The beauty of the wily Egyptian queen conquers the aging warrior Julius Caesar.

Handel was born in the city of Halle in Saxony and spent his early career in Germany and Italy before settling in London in 1712. British high society was then rabidly enthusiastic about opera "in the Italian style," which placed greater importance on the virtuosic gifts (as well as the box-office appeal) of star singers than on dramatic unity. Opera in London was usually sung in Italian rather than the vernacular as the Italian language, with its open vowel sounds and soft consonants, owned the double advantage of being easier to sing and sounding more fashionable than the King's English. As musical director of the Academy of Music, a consortium of noblemen formed to raise capital necessary for regular opera performances, Handel presented the most important European singers in their London debuts, composing operas which introduced his new artists with theatrical flourish.

Handel's *Giulio Cesare*, the sensation of London's 1724 winter season, centers on Julius Caesar's admiration of the bewitching young Egyptian queen Cleopatra. Handel filled the major roles with an all-star cast, most of them Italian-born. The widowed Roman matron Cornelia was played by the popular contralto Anastasia Robinson, a charming, dignified lady who retired from the stage within the year to begin a clandestine marriage to the Earl of Peterborough. In the role of her son Sesto was mezzo-soprano Margherita Durastanti, an artist great in many ways whose unkind nickname was "l'elefante."

Handel's first Cleopatra was Francesca Cuzzoni, a young woman of seraphic voice and devilish temper whose intractability was so fierce that the composer once threatened her with defenestration during a rehearsal. Cuzzoni was famous for her impeccable intonation and radiant purity of sound, but only her vocal charms justified her colossal fee of £2000 per annum; her figure was thick and dumpy and her face inexpressive. (Cuzzoni's career ended ignominiously when her precious voice was spent. Harried by creditors, she died in Bologna in 1770, by then a penurious buttonmaker.)

Julius Caesar himself was performed by the castrato Senesino. A powerful actor and penetrating singer, Senesino also created the title roles in *Ottone* (1723), *Siroe* (1728), and *Orlando* (1733) for Handel, who admired his voice but deplored his arrogance and volatility. The castrati were the rock stars of their era. These men, whose unbroken voices were preserved artificially by surgery before puberty, were a regular feature of operatic life in the eighteenth century. They combined male lung power and strength with female flexibility and tonal brilliance and enjoyed febrile adoration from their audiences. The practice of creating castrati gradually died out, a victim of changing musical tastes; the last important singer to practice the castrato's art was Giovanni Battista Velluti, who retired in 1830. In modern revivals of operas containing roles for castrati, the music is either transposed into a lower range or (more suitably) sung by counter-tenor or mezzo-soprano.

Giulio Cesare

Opera in 3 Acts

by

George Frideric Handel

ORPHÉE ET EURYDICE

Opera in 3 Acts

by

CHRISTOPH WILLIBALD VON GLUCK

(1714–1787)

Libretto: RANIERI DE' CALZABIGI
Premiere: VIENNA, BURGTHEATER; OCTOBER 5, 1762
Premiere French version: PARIS; AUGUST 2, 1774

Fittingly enough for a composer who spent much of his career chopping down entrenched operatic conventions, Christoph Willibald von Gluck was born into a family of foresters. An insatiable love for music took him from the tall woods of the Palatinate in Germany to the theatres of Milan, where his first opera *Artaserse* was born on the day after Christmas in 1741. Gluck traveled extensively throughout Europe in the following decade, winning praise for his compositions and marrying extremely well (to a bride half his age) before settling in Vienna in 1752. It was there that Gluck, by now the composer of almost a dozen operas, was introduced to Ranieri de' Calzabigi, an erstwhile business partner of Casanova and a protégé of Madame de Pompadour. Calzabigi presented Gluck with a libretto on the classical legend of Orpheus, the Thracian poet and singer granted the privilege of descending to Hades to return his cherished wife, Eurydice, back to the land of the living. It was a subject well suited to the composer's growing taste for "semplicità, verità, e naturalezza."

By the mid-eighteenth century, most operas were burdened by overly complicated plots, fussy music, unbelievable characters, and star singers bent on demonstrating their gifts at the expense of the drama. Gluck's "reform" operas sought to return the form to the model of classical simplicity. Gluck's music expressed the human emotions of Calzabigi's libretto; it neither stopped the action nor smothered it with ornament, instead fusing song, dance, mime, and poetry into a sublimely harmonious whole. The composer was later to state his objectives directly in the famous foreword to his opera *Alceste* (1767) and maintained his reformist stance in his later works.

Gluck's first Orfeo, Gaetano Guadagni, was a singing actor cut from a plainer cloth than his virtuoso predecessors. A contralto castrato who started his career in *burletta* and *opera buffa*, precursors of modern musical comedy, Guadagni was slim, comely, and intelligent. His natural gifts impressed Handel, who wrote the role of *Theodora*'s converted Roman centurion Didymus for him, and the staggeringly celebrated English actor David Garrick, who took Guadagni on as a private pupil. Guadagni undertook years of earnest study to re-form himself into a "serious" artist, emerging with a suitably grave demeanor and a much improved vocal technique. His strength of purpose made him an ideal interpreter of Gluck, who worked closely with him on the creation of *Orfeo* (1762) and *Telemacho* (1765).

Gluck brought an expanded *Orfeo* to Paris in 1774 as *Orphée et Eurydice*, a vehicle for the *haut-contre* (higher than high) tenor Joseph Legros. Regarded as clumsy and awkward before he worked under Gluck's insightful, supportive coaching, Legros was transformed into the paradigm of noble sincerity as *Orphée*. The tenor maintained a profitable working relationship with Gluck for many years, creating important roles in *Iphigénie en Aulide* (1774), *Iphigénie en Tauride* (1779), and the revision of *Alceste* (1776) before he retired from the stage at the age of forty-four, his stature as an artist at last overwhelmed by his increasing girth.

Orphée et Eurydice
The poet Orpheus's love for his wife, Eurydice, brings her back from Hades.

Orphée et Eurydice

Opera in 3 Acts
by

Christoph Willibald von Gluck

Le Nozze di Figaro

Opera in 4 Acts
by

Wolfgang Amadeus Mozart
(1756–1791)

Libretto: Lorenzo Da Ponte,
after Beaumarchais' comedy *La folle journée, ou Le mariage de Figaro*
Premiere: Vienna, Burgtheater; May 1, 1786

Wolfgang Amadeus Mozart first excercised his extraordinarily fecund musical imagination as an infant prodigy. He started composing at the age of five and at six began a series of concert tours to the courts of Europe. In 1767, when he was eleven and a half, his opera *Apollo et Hyacinthus* was performed as an intermission entertainment in Salzburg; before his twentieth birthday, there were to be eight more Mozart operas, as well as two dozen symphonies and an astonishing number of chamber pieces, vocal music, and concerti. The most important operatic works of Mozart's next decade were *Idomeneo, Re di Creta* (1781), an *opera seria* written on commission from the Elector of Bavaria, and *Die Entführung aus dem Serail* (1782).

Le Nozze di Figaro (1786) is a lusty but sophisticated comedy set in the Seville palace of Count Almaviva on the eve of his valet Figaro's wedding to the maid Susanna. The original play by Pierre Beaumarchais had made strong political points by emphasizing the venality of its aristocratic characters. Mozart's opera gave masters and servants equally human dimension, ending the plot's comedy of sexual intrigue with a masterstroke of insight: before the wronged Countess Almaviva answers her errant husband's plea for pardon, there is a split second of silence before she dissolves into forgiveness, suspending him (and the audience) over a heart-stopping chasm of doubt.

A successful production of *Le Nozze di Figaro* in Prague brought Mozart an opera commission there for the following season. *Don Giovanni* (1787), the story of a dissolute rake and the lives he touches, is neither comedy nor tragedy but a *dramma giocoso* (jocular drama), combining elements of both in an enticingly flammable union. Mozart's Don is a sociopathic seducer who laughs, loves, and leaves without a backward glance until dragged to hell unrepentant. The music for each of his ladies is charged with a uniquely appropriate sexual energy: a militaristic vengeance aria for the cold and haughty Donna Anna, a mellifluent rondo to reflect the pulsing bundle of contradictions within Donna Elvira, and a pair of ripely tender love songs for the nubile peasant girl Zerlina.

Mozart's librettist for *Le Nozze di Figaro*, *Don Giovanni,* and *Così fan tutte* (1790) was the incorrigibly libidinous Lorenzo Da Ponte, a Venetian who was the poet to the Imperial Theatres in Vienna. A promising seminarian until adultery caused his expulsion, the urbane and witty Da Ponte loved to mix business with pleasure and frequently cast his petulant mistress Adriana Gabrieli, known as "La Ferrarese," in leading roles. (Mozart was heard to grumble loudly when she was given Susanna in the 1789 Vienna revival of *Figaro* but still composed two new arias for her.) After the poet was dismissed from court service in 1791, he settled in London, remaining there until he emigrated to America in 1805, much to the frustration of his numerous creditors. When he was in his seventies, Da Ponte joined the faculty of Columbia University as a professor of Italian and published a racy four-volume autobiography. He remained active as a musical elder statesman and opera manager until his death at eighty-nine.

Above:
Don Giovanni (1787)

Opposite:
Le Nozze di Figaro
The Countess Almaviva mourns the
passing of her husband's affections.

Le Nozze di Figaro

Opera in 4 Acts

by

WOLFGANG AMADEUS MOZART

DIE ZAUBERFLÖTE
(THE MAGIC FLUTE)
Singspiel in 2 Acts
by
WOLFGANG AMADEUS MOZART
(1756–1791)

Libretto: EMANUEL SCHIKANEDER
Premiere: VIENNA, THEATER AUF DER WIEDEN; SEPTEMBER 30, 1791

The last year of Mozart's short life contained the premieres of two new operas. Formal composition was begun first on *Die Zauberflöte*, a commission from Emanuel Schikaneder, the actor-manager of Vienna's Theater auf der Wieden. The work was written as a *singspiel* (song-play), a German style of theatre employing spoken dialogue to connect musical numbers that Mozart had earlier used to coruscating effect in *Die Entführung aus dem Serail* (1782), a comedy set in a Turkish harem. The libretto for *Die Zauberflöte* was constructed by Schikaneder, a superb singing comedian who wrote the plum part of the befeathered bird catcher Papageno for himself.

Mozart broke off work on *Die Zauberflöte* to speed through the completion of *La Clemenza di Tito*, a formal *opera seria* scheduled for the National Theatre in Prague to celebrate the coronation of the Holy Roman Emperor Leopold II as King of Bohemia. (The Bohemian celebrations, one of several coronations and installations in the rather broad multinational Empire, were aptly timed, as Leopold would be dead within the year.) Mozart had considered an opera on the Roman Emperor Titus as early as 1789, but when the formal commission for the work did not arrive until seven weeks before the announced premiere, *Tito*'s final composition became a matter of some urgency. Mozart's pupil Franz Xaver Süssmayr (later to finish Mozart's posthumous *Requiem*) completed the recitatives and some of the arias. Distaste for the *opera seria* form (already moribund in Mozart's day) made sightings of *Tito* rare in the nineteenth and early twentieth centuries, but the work prospered in its early years. *La Clemenza di Tito* became the first Mozart opera to be heard in London when the luscious Mrs. Elizabeth Billington, England's first international star, consented to step into the slippers of the bloodthirsty Vitellia at the King's Theatre (1806).

Less than a month after the September 6 premiere of *Tito* in Prague, Mozart conducted the first performance of *Die Zauberflöte* in Vienna. *Die Zauberflöte* is an enigmatic comedy, its character interaction supported by a symbolic substructure based in the rituals of Freemasonry. Set in mythic Egypt, the plot pits the beneficent Sarastro, grand master of the mysteries of Isis, against the forces of darkness as personified by the malevolent Queen of the Night. Although the Queen brandishes a fearsome dagger, it is the altitudinous tessitura of her two big arias, ascending more than once to high F, that has scared sopranos witless in the two centuries since the role was created by Mozart's dauntless sister-in-law, Josepha Weber. *Die Zauberflöte* brought welcome financial security to Schikaneder, whose theatre had been in shaky estate, but arrived too late in Mozart's career to rescue him from poverty.

Exhausted by overwork and illness, Mozart died in Vienna on December 5, 1791, and was buried in an unmarked grave. He was thirty-five. Contrary to the theories espoused by Rimsky-Korsakov's 1898 opera *Mozart i Salieri* and Peter Shaffer's play *Amadeus*, Mozart was not poisoned or driven mad by his rival Antonio Salieri. A bout of rheumatic fever in 1784 had weakened a constitution already far from robust, and the unheated poverty in which Mozart spent his final days was scarcely conducive to good health.

Die Zauberflöte
The vengeance of hell blackens the heart of the Queen of the Night.

Die Zauberflöte

Singspiel in 2 Acts
by

Wolfgang Amadeus Mozart

NORMA

Opera in 2 Acts
by

VINCENZO BELLINI
(1801–1835)

Libretto: LUIGI ROMANI, AFTER ALEXANDRE SOUMET'S TRAGEDY *NORMA,*
OU L'INFANTICIDE
Premiere: MILAN, TEATRO ALLA SCALA; DECEMBER 26, 1831

Top:
Semiramide (1823)
Gioacchino Rossini (1792–1868)

Above:
Anna Bolena (1830)
Gaetano Donizetti (1797–1848)

Opposite:
Norma
The high priestess of the Druids
mounts the pyre as a sacrificial victim.

The principal Italian opera composers of the Romantic Era were Gioacchino Rossini, Gaetano Donizetti, and Vincenzo Bellini. The group label *"bel canto* operas," often assigned to their works, is an inaccurate term; the phrase, literally translated as "beautiful song," more properly defines a style of singing than a school of composing. *Bel canto* singers achieve dramatic expressiveness through vocal technique, their breath control commanding both easy legato phrasing and rapid coloratura ornamentation of melody. While the art of *bel canto* was perfected by the mid-1800s, the style continued to be influential long afterward, eventually marking the compositional style of Verdi, Wagner, and Puccini. It is still taught today.

Rossini, Donizetti, and Bellini were a highly individual trio. Rossini was born first and died last; his more than thirty-five operas (all composed before he was forty) include the zesty comedy *Il barbiere di Siviglia* (1816), a Scottish love story, *La donna del lago* (1819), and the nationalistic pageantry of *Guillaume Tell* (1829). *Tell* was the final stage work for Rossini, who lived another thirty-nine years in almost silent retirement. Donizetti, born a few years later, was a master at showcasing the great singers of his own day and of succeeding generations; his *L'elisir d'amore* (1832) and *Lucia di Lammermoor* (1835) have enjoyed unbroken popularity since their premieres.

Bellini, who died at thirty-three, has the smallest oeuvre of the triumvirate but wrote a truly glorious role for the opera *Norma* (1831). The daughter of the Arch-Druid Oroveso, the high priestess Norma betrays her vow of chastity for the love of the Roman proconsul Pollione. When her guilty secret (and her two half-Roman children) are discovered, Norma offers herself as a sacrificial victim to the gods of war and mounts the funeral pyre. Noble yet passionate, Norma requires from her interpreter brute strength, emotional quickness, and personal majesty in equal measure.

Norma is the soprano's *Hamlet*—which is a graceful way of saying that most critics prefer ladies who no longer sing the role to those who currently do so. The greatest Norma may have been the first: Giuditta Pasta, by all accounts an uncommonly persuasive singer and an actress of magisterial power. Bellini's priestess tested even Pasta's considerable resources to the maximum and its conquest may have cost her dearly; after singing the opera more than thirty times in its first season, the soprano's voice lost much of its quality and control.

An era which valued interpretative genius far above rational thought was a fertile breeding ground for prima donnas, and Pasta led a phalanx of younger singers into immortality. Her talented juniors included Giulia Grisi, a raven-haired *intrigante* who was Queen Victoria's favorite singer; the tempestuous, meltingly pretty Maria Malibran, mortally injured in a riding accident at twenty-eight; and Spanish soprano Isabella Colbran, the grand and voluptuous favorite of the King of Naples and of Rossini, who married her and wrote many roles for her, among them the Babylonian queen *Semiramide* (1823). The highly combustible Giuseppina de Begnis preferred to bestow her favors seriatim upon the King of Sicily and Donizetti, creating the latter's *Maria Stuarda* (1834) and nearly delaying its premiere when she settled a rehearsal dispute with such finality that her co-star was confined to bed for a fortnight's recuperation. Such tantrums in the name of art were the norm for the Romantic Era, when heroines often went spectacularly, wildly mad when cornered. Even Anne Boleyn, whom history tells us was quite self-possessed, becomes prettily unhinged before she meets the headsman's sword in Donizetti's *Anna Bolena* (1830).

N O R M A

Opera in 2 Acts
by
Vincenzo Bellini

L'Africaine

Opera in 5 Acts

by

Giacomo Meyerbeer

(1791–1864)

Libretto: Eugène Scribe
Premiere: Paris, Opéra; April 28, 1865

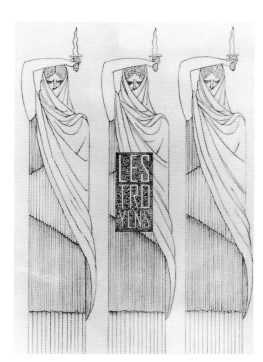

French Grand Opera (its initial capitals necessary to salute the attendant spectacle of the form) had its beginnings in the Paris of Napoleon Bonaparte, when vast pageants drawn from classical subjects were produced by Jean-François Le Sueur (*Ossian*, 1804) and Gaspare Spontini (*La Vestale*, 1807). These operas have a formal grandeur similar to the contemporaneous paintings of Jacques-Louis David, depicting individuals in private crises against an historical background, with the glory that was Rome often used as a celebratory metaphor for the far-reaching ambitions of the new emperor.

Throughout the Bourbon Restoration and into the period of the Second Empire, Grand Opera continued to find favor with the Parisians, who liked their operas king-sized no matter who occupied their throne. The conventions of the genre included ballets, huge choruses in parade formation, noble protagonists with terrible secrets, opulent ceremonials (often interrupted by bad news), and rafter-rattling natural disasters on the order of conflagration, flood, or earthquake. Invasion and revolution were also favored plot devices, with both sometimes used in the same opera.

Grand Opera reached its apotheosis in France in the works of Giacomo Meyerbeer. Born into a prosperous German-Jewish family near Berlin, the former Jakob Liebmann Meyer Beer had his early operas produced in Munich, Dresden, Venice, and Milan before marking his shrewdly planned conquest of Paris with *Robert le Diable* in 1831. *Robert* was Meyerbeer's first collaboration with French librettist Eugène Scribe, whose infallible instinct for Parisian box office appeal furnished sprawling, episodic storylines calculated to provide the latest in dramatic thrills and eye-filling tableaux. Such effects typically did little to advance the plot. *Robert le Diable* featured a spooky, show-stopping ballet with a corps of dead nuns, while *Le Prophète* (1849), an historical epic centered on a sixteenth-century Anabaptist uprising, cools down for an interlude of ice skating in Act III.

L'Africaine is a highly fictionalized gloss on the life of Portuguese explorer Vasco da Gama, the first European to reach India. He is loved by Inez, a noblewoman, and by the captured slave Selika, who is an Indian queen despite the opera's title. (Such details are best ignored when discussing Meyerbeer.) There is an onstage shipwreck and massacre, a Hindu temple wedding, and hours of beautiful music before Selika commits suicide by inhaling the lethal perfume of the flowering mancanilla tree as da Gama sails for home.

Meyerbeer was admired more by his audiences than by the musical press, who classified him as a purveyor of sensation for sensation's sake. His highly original orchestrations and supple vocal writing are still striking today, when expensive production demands, large casts, and the modern critical community's appetite for operatic leanness have made revivals of Meyerbeer's enormous spectacles rare.

Meyerbeer's brilliant contemporary Hector Berlioz, underrated during his lifetime, has now achieved a posthumous reputation greater than that of his more successful colleague. Berlioz's visionary epic *Les Troyens*, based on the Roman poet Virgil's story of the Trojan War, was never performed complete during his lifetime. The truncated version (centering on the *Trojans at Carthage* section) given by the Paris Théâtre Lyrique in 1863 disappointed Berlioz bitterly, and he died believing that his work would never be heard in its original form. *Les Troyens*, now regarded as one of opera's masterworks, was given its first full production in French at Covent Garden, London, in 1969, a century after the composer's death.

Above:
Les Troyens (comp. 1856–58)
Hector Berlioz (1803–1869)

Opposite:
L'Africaine
Selika is consumed by a celestial vision
of her god Brahma.

L'AfriCaIne

Opera in 5 Acts
by
Giacomo Meyerbeer

Tannhäuser und der Sängerkrieg auf Wartburg
(Tannhäuser and the Song Contest on the Wartburg)

Opera in 3 Acts

by

Richard Wagner
(1813–1883)

Libretto: Richard Wagner
Premiere: Dresden; October 19, 1845

No other composer has ever inspired the paradoxical combination of veneration and villification that constitutes the reputation of Richard Wagner, who changed the sound and texture of music in his generation and in the generations that followed him. He was a brilliant conductor, a visionary dramatist and poet who wrote his own lengthy librettos, a passionate man of the theatre knowledgeable in design, administration, and stage direction, the theorist of *gesamtkunstwerk* (the unified art work combining all arts), and a widely-read essayist whose influence was felt in literature, art, criticism, dietetics, social theory, and politics.

That Wagner was one of his century's giants in music and drama is unquestionable, but it is equally certain that Wagner was ruthless, vain and often petty, an arrogant spendthrift, an appalling husband, a childish lover, and an unapologetic racist and anti-Semite. A controversial figure in life, Wagner remains a social and musical lightning rod more than a century after his death.

Richard Wagner did not study music with any urgency until he was in his mid-teens. He later claimed that his inspiration was a performance of Beethoven's opera *Fidelio* in which the thrilling young prima donna Wilhelmine Schröder-Devrient sang Leonore with what Wagner called "almost satanic ardor." Schröder-Devrient later became one of Wagner's many financial patrons and was the first important singer to appear in his operas, creating Adriano in *Rienzi* (1842), Senta in *Der Fliegende Holländer* (1843) and Venus in *Tannhäuser* (1845). Wagner's first produced opera was *Das Liebesverbot* (1836), a setting of Shakespeare's *Measure for Measure*. It was a disaster, clouding his courtship and eventual marriage the same year to a rather pretty actress named Minna Planer.

Wagner and Minna's married life can be summed up in a sequence of three words: debt, arguments, and travel. Wagner would spend too much money, fight with Minna about it, and follow this with a change of address. (Wagner's most urgent flight came in the wake of the 1848 European revolutions, when unwise political choices forced him into exile in Switzerland.) Minna, whose own commitment to marriage was sometimes infirm, was gradually worn down by the frenetic level of her husband's extra-marital obsessions and was estranged from Wagner when she died in 1866.

Wagner's first three important operas concerned the redemptive power of love. In *Der Fliegende Holländer*, the visionary Senta leaps to her death in order to bring salvation to the soul of the condemned Dutchman. The minstrel knight Tannhäuser, who has enjoyed the heathen pleasures of the kingdom of Venus, is drawn back to spiritual grace through the influence of the chaste Elisabeth of Thuringia. In *Lohengrin* (1850), a knight in shining armor arrives by swan boat to act as champion for Elsa von Brabant, unjustly accused of her brother Gottfried's murder. Unbeknownst to all until the end of Act III is that the swan is really Gottfried, enchanted by the sorceress Ortrud until released by the intercession of Lohengrin's pure spirit.

Above:
Lohengrin (1850)

Opposite:
Tannhäuser
The minstrel knight Tannhäuser lives under the spell of Venus for a year and a day.

TANNHÄUSER

und der Sängerkrieg auf Wartburg

Opera in 3 Acts

by

RICHARD WAGNER

Die Meistersinger von Nürnberg
(THE MASTERSINGERS OF NUREMBERG)

Opera in 3 Acts

by

RICHARD WAGNER
(1813–1883)

Libretto: RICHARD WAGNER
Premiere: MUNICH; JUNE 21, 1868

Richard Wagner's posthumous reputation is swathed in such solemnity that most initiate Wagnerites are surprised to find that the great man wrote an opera with a happy ending. The romantic hero of the "human comedy" *Die Meistersinger* is the poet and singer Walther von Stolzing, who tries for acceptance in the Nuremberg Guild of Mastersingers with a novel type of song. Walther wins the song contest (and the hand of the lovely Eva) with the assistance of the cobbler Hans Sachs. Wagner saw Walther's role as a champion of new music as analogous to his own, and in the character of the pedantic clerk Sixtus Beckmesser, Walther's chief rival, he drew a cutting portrait of Viennese writer Eduard Hanslick, one of his own severest critics.

Wagner began sketching *Die Meistersinger* in 1845. He resumed work on the piece in the early 1860s, finishing the score in October 1867 at Triebschen, the house near Lucerne then providing him refuge from his powerful critics at the Bavarian court of his patron, King Ludwig II. At the first performance of *Die Meistersinger* in June 1868, Wagner shared the royal box at the Nationaltheater with the king, acknowledging the opening night ovation for the work as if he were a monarch himself. Munich society—and the Munich press—were outraged, and Wagner was much criticized and caricatured as an impossible egotist.

Additional drama simmered in the orchestra pit the night of the *Meistersinger* premiere. Conductor Hans von Bülow was court pianist to the king, an ardent supporter of Wagner's music, and the very obliging husband of Wagner's mistress Cosima, who had borne the composer two daughters but still remained very much Frau von Bülow. Cosima, twenty-four years Wagner's junior, was one of three love children resulting from the scandalous liaison between Comtesse Marie d'Agoult, the French writer, and composer Franz Liszt. (Liszt, an enthusiastic champion of Wagner's music who had conducted the first performance of *Lohengrin*, was much embarrassed by his daughter's marital irregularities, his own colorful past notwithstanding.) It was not until August 1870, more than a year after the birth of their third child, that Cosima finally married Richard Wagner.

Cosima was wed to Wagner for thirteen years and lived another forty-seven as his widow. She filled their decades apart by guarding her husband's work and reputation with a zeal that touched ferocity. The sanctity of Wagner's last opera *Parsifal* (1882) consumed her almost totally. *Parsifal* is rich with symbolism dealing with the Last Supper and Crucifixion of Jesus Christ and was intended by Wagner for performance only at Bayreuth. Cosima petitioned in vain to have the Bayreuth copyright on the work extended, and filed an (unsuccessful) injunction against the 1903 *Parsifal* at the Metropolitan Opera in New York. The singers who participated in that *Parsifal* (some of whom were distinguished Bayreuth veterans) were from that moment dead to the immovable Frau Wagner.

Above:
Parsifal (1882)

Opposite:
Die Meistersinger von Nürnberg
The victor's wreath of laurel and myrtle belongs to Walther von Stolzing.

Die Meistersinger von Nürnberg

Opera in 3 Acts
by
RICHARD WAGNER

DER RING DES NIBELUNGEN
(THE RING OF THE NIBELUNG)

A Stage-Festival Play for 3 Days & a Preliminary Evening

by

RICHARD WAGNER
(1813–1883)

Libretto: RICHARD WAGNER
Premiere: BAYREUTH, FESTSPIELHAUS; AUGUST 13, 14, 16, 17, 1876

If its four parts are considered as a single musical narrative, then Richard Wagner's *Der Ring des Nibelungen* (*The Ring Cycle*) is the longest opera in the standard repertory. The *Ring* has four component music dramas, each requiring an entire evening to perform. *Das Rheingold* (The Rhinegold), the shortest of the four, was considered by Wagner to be an explanatory prologue to the other three operas. *Die Walküre* (The Valkyrie) is the most popular of the *Ring* quartet and the one most frequently performed outside the rest of the cycle. The massive *Siegfried* is probably the least accessible *Ring* evening and the hardest to stage, requiring a tireless *heldentenor*, an extremely patient dramatic soprano (who sings for only the last twenty minutes of a five-hour evening), and a talking dragon. *Götterdämmerung* (The Twilight of the Gods) brings the cycle to a fiery close over eighteen hours after the performance began.

The greatness of the *Ring* is not just a matter of length. Its concept was revolutionary and its very spirit huge, combining myth and reality in a mighty saga of man, woman, and the gods. The construction and eventual presentation of the cycle occupied Wagner for more than twenty-five years. His reading of Norse and Teutonic myths—among these the Völsunga Saga and the Niebelungenlied—brought Wagner to start work on *Siegfrieds Tod* (Siegfried's Death) as early as 1848. Frustrated that he was unable to include the entire Siegfried story within the framework of a single dramatic work despite several re-drafts, Wagner started what Hollywood might call a "prequel," *Der Junge Siegfried*, which took his hero back further in time. It was then that Wagner re-thought the music drama as a tetralogy (or, more exactly, a trilogy with a prologue), completing the dramas (libretti) for *Die Walküre* and *Das Rheingold* by the fall of 1852 and then reworking the two Siegfried pieces into the beginnings of what would be the third and fourth operas of the projected cycle.

The scoring of the operas occupied Wagner until 1857, when he decided to put the cycle aside two-thirds of the way through *Siegfried*. It seemed unlikely that such a huge work, its staging requirements far beyond the capacity of any theatre in Europe, would ever be produced. During the twelve-year gap before work was resumed on the *Ring* Wagner kept himself occupied by accepting as many conducting engagements as he could, revising *Tannhäuser* for its notoriously unsuccessful Paris production (1861), composing *Tristan und Isolde* (1865) and *Die Meistersinger* (1868), spending more money than he could afford, and having several love affairs, both requited and otherwise.

In 1864, the newly crowned King Ludwig II of Bavaria (nicknamed "the Mad") took Wagner under his generous patronage, relieving the composer of his debts and sponsoring productions of his operas in Munich. Ludwig's financial sponsorship helped build a Festspielhaus (festival theatre) in the Franconian town of Bayreuth, designed according to Wagner's specifications with a raked auditorium, hidden orchestra pit, and exemplary acoustics. In 1876, *Das Rheingold* inaugurated both the theatre and the first complete presentation of the *Ring*, with productions of Wagner's other major works mounted in later seasons. The Bayreuth Festival remains active today, providing the world's Wagnerites with a place of pilgrimage every summer.

Der Ring des Nibelungen
Siegfried is subdued by the curse on the ring of the Nibelung.

DER RING DES NIBELUNGEN

A Stage-Festival Play for 3 Days
& a Preliminary Evening
by

RICHARD WAGNER

RIGOLETTO

Melodramma in 3 Acts

by

GIUSEPPE VERDI
(1813–1901)

Libretto: FRANCESCO MARIA PIAVE, AFTER VICTOR HUGO'S DRAMA *LE ROI S'AMUSE*
Premiere: VENICE, TEATRO LA FENICE; MARCH 11, 1851

Fate has a pleasant knack of putting geniuses in the right place at the right time. When Giuseppe Verdi's first opera, *Oberto, Conte de San Bonifacio*, was produced at La Scala, Milan, in the autumn of 1839, the great compositional voices of the previous generation in Italy were gradually falling silent. A few years earlier, Bellini had died, tragically young, in a suburb of Paris—the same city where Rossini lived in self-imposed retirement, his days as a theatre composer abruptly but irrevocably ended after the production of *Guillaume Tell* in 1829. By 1844, ill health would vanquish the exhaustingly prolific Gaetano Donizetti (still in burgeoning mid-career when *Oberto* was born) and Giuseppe Verdi would be recognized as Italy's leading young composer.

Twenty-six when his first opera was produced and then bought for publication by the prestigious House of Ricordi, Verdi almost stopped writing for the theatre before he was thirty. Verdi's daughter and son both succumbed to childhood illness within sixteen months of one another; less than a year later, in 1840, his beautiful young wife, Margherita Barezzi, died of rheumatic fever. Further crushed by the failure of his second opera, *Un Giorno di Regno* (1840), the young composer was unproductive for nearly a year. Verdi was drawn back to work by the psychological maneuvering of Bartolomeo Merelli, the director of La Scala, who tempted him successfully with Temistocle Solera's libretto *Nabucodonosor*. (Another spurt to Verdi's creativity was the beautiful prima donna Giuseppina Strepponi, who became his second wife in 1859.)

Now generally known as *Nabucco*, the opera was a smashing success from its first performance in March 1842. *Nabucco* deals with the captivity of the Hebrews in Old Testament Babylon, a condition which had great resonance for Verdi's fellow Italians then under occupation by the Austrians. The Hebrew prisoners' chorus "Va, pensiero" was played everywhere and became the anthem of those who wished for a free Italy. (The composer's very name eventually became an acronym for "Vittorio Emmanuele, Re d'Italia," the rallying cry to unify the Italian peninsula under the rule of Victor Emmanuel II, the King of Sardinia.)

Success emboldened Verdi, who would write fourteen operas in the next nine years, among them *Ernani* (1844), *Macbeth* (1847), and *Luisa Miller* (1849). In 1851, he produced *Rigoletto*, a work of profound majesty and visceral strength that began the great middle period of his career. In his early operas, Verdi had honored the conventions of Italian opera; with *Rigoletto* he transformed them. The characters are drawn with insight and compassion and maintain their musical individuality in ensembles as well as solos, nowhere more imaginatively than in the magnificent last act quartet that captures four voices in a blend of contradictory emotions.

Rigoletto is an embittered, hunchbacked jester in the court of the Duke of Mantua, a libertine who seduces the jester's daughter Gilda. When the enraged father hires a professional assassin to dispatch the Duke, it is Gilda who is killed by mistake. The relationship between daughter and father at the heart of *Rigoletto* is a motif often revisited in the operas of Verdi, its frequency made poignant by the knowledge that happy fatherhood was an estate that the composer longed for but never achieved.

Rigoletto
The jester masks his true bitterness.

Rigoletto

Melodramma in 3 Acts
by

GIUSEPPE VERDI

Un Ballo in Maschera
(A MASKED BALL)
Opera in 3 Acts
by
Giuseppe Verdi
(1813–1901)

Libretto: Antonio Somma, based on a libretto by Eugène Scribe
Premiere: Rome, Teatro Apollo; February 17, 1859

The four-decade progression of Verdi masterworks that began with the premiere of *Rigoletto* continued with *Il Trovatore* (1853). The conventional wisdom for enjoying this dark Spanish romance dictates ignoring its rather twisted plot and savoring its thrilling music, keyed up by one of Verdi's supreme roles for tenor: the warrior troubadour Manrico, a gentleman as handy with a sword as he is with a high C. Manrico's companions in song include the high-minded noblewoman Leonora (a soprano, of course), the dastardly Count di Luna (a loveless baritone, as all truly first-class opera villains are), a chorus of anvil-hammering gypsies, and the aged *zingara* Azucena, who may or may not be Manrico's mother. (Most operas with impossibly convoluted storylines feature either a gypsy or an elderly mezzo-soprano in a key role. Azucena fits both descriptions.)

Forty-six days after *Il Trovatore* opened in Rome, *La Traviata* bowed in Venice. The new opera was based upon *La dame aux camélias*, a drama borrowed by Alexandre Dumas fils from his own liaison with Marie Duplessis, a short-lived princess of the 1840s Parisian *demi-monde*. *La Traviata* offers a simple but sad twist on boy-meets-girl: Alfredo Germont, a callow youth of good family, falls hard and fast for Violetta Valéry, a glamorous courtesan in precarious health who succumbs to a combination of consumption, social pressure, and untrammeled masochism.

The birth of Verdi's *Un Ballo in Maschera* (1859) was nearly wrecked by censorship problems. Its subject—the murder of a king by political insurgents—was admittedly controversial, but Verdi underestimated the intransigence of the censors in Naples, where *Una vendetta in domino*, as the opera was originally titled, was scheduled for its first performance. Antonio Somma's libretto was based on the real-life assassination of the Swedish king at a Stockholm Opera House masquerade in 1792. The historical Gustavus III was a thick-skinned autocrat who cheated death for almost two weeks after being shot in the back by Captain Jacob Anckarström. The opera libretto does the monarch in with a quick stab to the ribs, his murder the result of a jealous husband's rage.

The Neapolitan censors of Verdi's day were unusually jumpy because of a recent assassination attempt, in which French Emperor Napoleon III was almost murdered on his way to the Opéra. They requested numerous amendments to Verdi's text and score before permitting production in Naples: the king was to become an ordinary citizen, the count's adulterous wife changed into his sister, any suggestion of a ball was to be eliminated (with any murder taking place offstage), and the locale was to be moved back in history, preferably to the fourteenth century. Verdi was especially angered by the suggestion that the mischievous page boy Oscar (a traditional "trouser role" in which a youthful male character is impersonated by a woman) be re-written as a middle-aged soldier. The composer withdrew the unproduced opera from Naples in disgust.

When a Roman impresario produced *Ballo* the following year, the only major change required in the text was that the locale be non-European. Thus was the Swedish ball moved to Boston, Massachusetts, in the seventeenth century and Gustavus III and Count Anckarström transformed into Riccardo, the English Royal Governor, and Renato, his "Creole adviser." Whatever the setting, Verdi's score retains its glory, leavening the tragic grandeur of its love story with dashes of fanciful comedy.

Un Ballo in Maschera
Husband, wife, and king meet at a masquerade dance.

Un Ballo in Maschera

Un Ballo in Maschera

Opera in 3 Acts

by

GIUSEPPE VERDI

AÏDA

Opera in 4 Acts
by
GIUSEPPE VERDI
(1813–1901)

Libretto: ANTONIO GHISLANZONI
Premiere: CAIRO OPERA HOUSE, EGYPT; DECEMBER 24, 1871

Verdi's later career was marked by periods of musical silence that invariably ended with the premiere of a new masterpiece. His term in the new Italian parliament allowed Verdi the time for only the chilly *La Forza del Destino* (1862), first given in St. Petersburg. *Don Carlos*, an historical drama that for many represents the zenith of the French Grand Opera style, bowed in Paris in 1867. The maestro's most popular opera—and by some tallies the most popular opera ever—was the Egyptian epic *Aïda* (1871), which made its debut in Cairo before taking a triumphal march through the opera houses of Europe.

Aïda, set in Memphis and Thebes in the age of the Pharaohs, reaffirmed Verdi's gift for shaping complex characters able to maintain their musical and dramatic identity no matter how vast the panorama of their surroundings. In the second act of *Aïda* a stupendous victory pageant before the Temple of Ammon celebrates the Egyptian nation's deliverance from the invading Ethiopians. As an endless parade of soldiers, chariots, musicians, dancing girls, priests and priestesses, sacred vessels, and (should the budget of the opera house allow) a caparisoned menagerie of stallions, camels, and elephants pass in review before the King and his haughty daughter Amneris, Verdi unerringly directs the audience's eye and ear toward the slave girl Aïda. No common slave, she is a captive Ethiopian princess, torn between her grief for her defeated nation and her secret love for Radamès, leader of the victorious Egyptian troops. The great ensemble roars its fabulous hymns of triumph, calling on gods and the king for revenge, but it is Aïda's voice—shot through with anguish and love—that gives the tragedy of war a human face.

The opera ends with a *coup de théâtre* constructed with the bare simplicity of genius. When the Egyptian soldier Radamès is condemned to be buried alive beneath the Temple of Vulcan, Aïda chooses to die with her lover rather than face life without him. Aïda and Radamès slowly expire in their subterranean tomb, hailing the ecstasy of immortal love as the priests and priestesss in the temple hall above them chant an invocation to the creator god Phtha. The voices of the lovers and the priests gradually give way to the solitary grief of the King's daughter Amneris, who prostrates herself upon the stone that seals Radamès's crypt, brokenly begging the gods to bring peace to the warrior dying in the chamber below.

When Verdi was in his late sixties he began the most significant artistic partnership of his life with the librettist/composer Arrigo Boito, a sardonic wit almost thirty years his junior with an aristocratic air and a roving eye. Their first joint project, a revision of Verdi's 1857 opera *Simon Boccanegra*, was a critical victory for both partners when unveiled at La Scala in 1881. For the rest of his career, Verdi had a librettist whose artistry approached his own.

At seventy—an age when his innummerable career laurels would have provided quite a comfortable resting place—Verdi began work on *Otello*, Boito's trenchant distillation of Shakespeare's drama. Received with almost hysterical approbation at its La Scala world premiere in 1887 (Verdi himself had more than a dozen curtain calls), *Otello* is one of the maestro's finest scores. It would have been a fitting end to a great career had Verdi not astonished the world with one final masterwork when he was almost eighty years old. In *Falstaff* (1893), Verdi and Boito brought Shakespeare's fat knight and all his delicious naughtiness to musical life in a relaxed, breezy comedy glowing with the shimmer of an autumn twilight.

Above:
Otello (1887)

Opposite:
Aïda
As her warrior hero dies, the Pharaoh's daughter prays for peace.

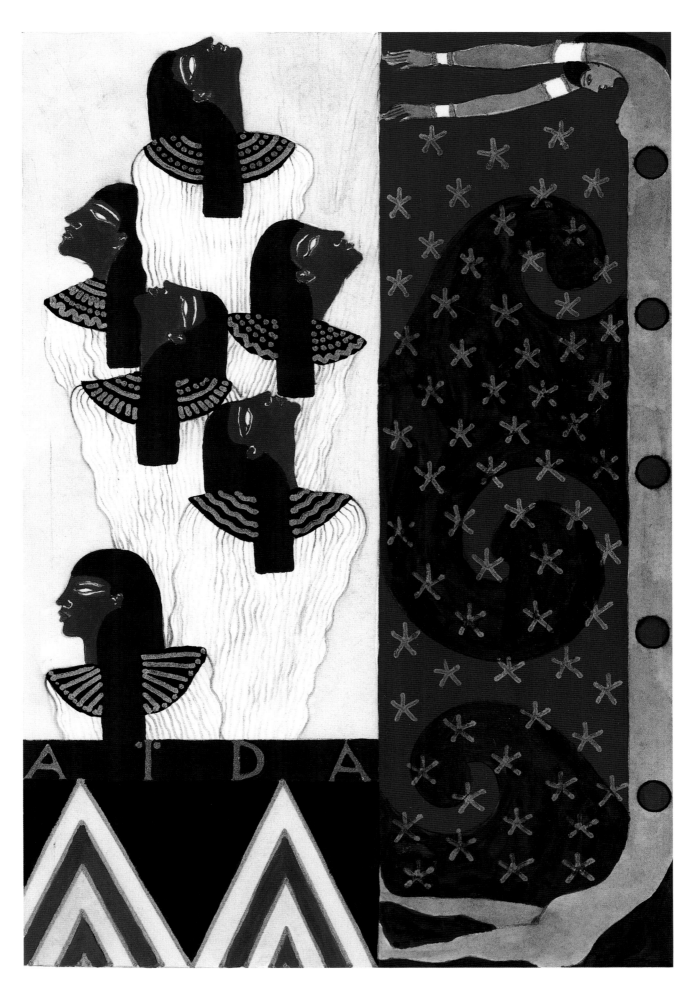

AÏDA

Opera in 4 Acts

by

GIUSEPPE VERDI

La Bohème

Opera in 4 Acts

by

Giacomo Puccini

(1858–1924)

Libretto: Giuseppe Giacosa and Luigi Illica, after Henri Murger's novel
Scènes de la vie de Bohème
Premiere: Turin, Teatro Regio; February 1, 1896

Just as the beginning of Giuseppe Verdi's career coincided with the waning of the Romantic masters Rossini, Donizetti, and Bellini, so did Giacomo Puccini emerge as Verdi's own heir in the Italian lyric tradition as the nineteenth century was ending. The son of a Donizetti pupil, Puccini was born in the Tuscan city of Lucca and studied in Milan under Amilcare Ponchielli, the composer of the melodramatic *La Gioconda*, a staple of Italian opera since its premiere in 1876.

The granitic echo of Ponchielli is audible in Puccini's earliest operas, *Le Villi* (1884) and *Edgar* (1889), both missteps that labored strenuously to maintain an atmosphere of medieval romance. The maestro found his true voice with *Manon Lescaut* (1893), a bold, full-bodied setting of the Abbé Prévost novel previously adapted for the opera by Daniel-François Auber (1856) and Jules Massenet (1884). The Manon of Puccini may lack the champagne delicacy of Massenet's quintessentially French heroine, but she owns a ripely Italianate vitality that is equally compelling.

La Bohème (1896), now entering its second century in the international repertory, is a one-size-fits-all-opera-companies work. A dexterously constructed and intimately focused musical story, with its central quartet of attractive young lovers, makes *Bohème* an ideal work for smaller theatres (and smaller-voiced singers), while its scenes of Paris's Latin Quarter teem with enough life to fill the greatest stages of the world. At the heart of the opera's appeal is the doomed seamstress Mimì, who can still chisel a chip in a heart of stone with her pained, tubercular farewell to the jealous poet Rodolfo. (In the interest of full disclosure, it would be politic to admit here that a woman in love in a Puccini opera is usually living on borrowed time.) Operatic highbrows have always been suspicious of Puccini's sentimentality, but it is an essential part of his uncanny genius for pleasing audiences, a prescience that is the equal of any figure in theatrical history.

Critical reception to the first production of *La Bohème* was fairly cool but audiences—who in Puccini's day often had the good sense to ignore critics—responded by filling the auditorium of Turin's Teatro Regio whenever the new piece was played. The future of *La Bohème* looked doubtful, however, until two things put Puccini's opera on the international map. The first was a production in Palermo, Sicily, in April 1896 that was greeted with such feverish, unstoppable joy on opening night—it was said that the audience refused to leave the theatre until all of Act Four was encored—that newspapers throughout Italy carried the story, priceless publicity that piqued the curiosity of the nation's operaphiles. The second was the championship of *Bohème* by Nellie Melba, the *prima donna assoluta* of London's Covent Garden. Born Helen Mitchell in a suburb of Melbourne, Australia, Melba's silver voice and cast-iron ego had made her the greatest soprano in Europe, but the coloratura works and French repertoire that had established her name were beginning to slip from fashion as the nineteenth century closed. The great lady needed a new vehicle to keep her celebrity moving forward (the Darwinian theory of survival through evolution applying to divas as well as the lower orders of animal life) and *La Bohème*'s Mimì proved to be an ideal Melba role. After her seal of approval established *Bohème* in New York, in London and around the world, Melba reigned as Mimì for almost forty years. Her grave bears as its inscription Mimì's words to her lover: "Addio, senza rancor."

La Bohème
The seamstress Mimì enchants the poet Rodolfo by candlelight.

La Bohème

Opera in 4 Acts
by
GIACOMO PUCCINI

Tosca

Opera in 3 Acts
by

Giacomo Puccini
(1858–1924)

Libretto: Giuseppe Giacosa and Luigi Illica, after Sardou's drama *La Tosca*
Premiere: Rome, Teatro Costanzi; January 14, 1900

Giacomo Puccini was a man of good heart but bad habits. He was an unapologetic and lusty gourmand, favoring rich dishes of fresh game washed down with copious draughts of rough wine and followed by vast platters of sweets; gradually the skinny music student from Lucca swelled into a sleek and imposing maestro with a temperamental digestion and troublesome teeth. Puccini slept irregularly, choosing to work through the night at his upright piano, fortified by strong coffee and packets of Turkish cigarettes, and leaving his study at dawn to go duck shooting. Cycling, motoring, and sailing were among Puccini's other outdoor activities, but his favorite sport was the pursuit and conquest of beautiful ladies. The composer planned his amorous pleasures tirelessly and democratically, as likely to dally with a chambermaid as with a prima donna while his ferociously jealous common-law wife fumed. (In 1904, the Puccinis finally married, thus legitimizing both their union of twenty years and their son of seventeen.)

After *Bohème* was established, each announcement of a new Puccini opera was an eagerly awaited (and relentlessly scrutinized) event in the world of music. As fame brought increased pressure upon the composer to match previous successes, Puccini agonized over his choice of opera subjects, considering a library of titles (and picking apart stacks of libretto drafts) before eventually rejecting them. A partial list of the projects Puccini toyed with and abandoned—many of them the bases for successful musicals or operas by later composers—includes Victor Hugo's novels *Notre Dame de Paris* and *Les Misérables*, a historical drama on the life of Buddha, Maurice Maeterlinck's verse drama *Pelléas et Mélisande*, Tolstoy's *Anna Karenina*, *The Last Days of Pompeii* by Edward Bulwer-Lytton, *Lorna Doone*, and *Rip Van Winkle*. The composer was fascinated by the doomed French queen Marie Antoinette (and a libretto on her last days called *The Austrian Woman*) and by Nancy, the gallant prostitute of Charles Dickens's *Oliver Twist*, but neither lady was to become a Puccini heroine.

It was *La Tosca*, one of the many historical dramas that French playwright Victorien Sardou tailored for the ineffably flamboyant shoulders of the great actress Sarah Bernhardt, that provided Puccini with an opera libretto to succeed *La Bohème*. Floria Tosca is a Roman prima donna embroiled in a cloak-and-dagger mix of Bonapartists, monarchists, and secret police, her nakedly emotional temperament pitted against the oily skullduggery of Baron Scarpia, opera's sexiest villain. When Tosca is trapped by the baron, she murders him, later escaping capture by jumping to her own death from the roof of the prison castle of Sant'Angelo. Before hurling herself into space, the diva cries "Scarpia, we shall meet again before God!" It is a fitting epitaph, for unlike her sisters in an earlier operatic era, Tosca doesn't go mad. She gets even.

Tosca
Alone with Scarpia, Tosca watches
and waits.

Tosca

Opera in 3 Acts
by
GIACOMO PUCCINI

Madama Butterfly

Opera in 3 Acts

by

Giacomo Puccini

(1858–1924)

Libretto: Giuseppe Giacosa and Luigi Illica,
after David Belasco's drama and a story by John Luther Long
Premiere: Milan, Teatro alla Scala; February 17, 1904

It is doubtful that any new contender will emerge before the year 2000 to displace *Madama Butterfly* (1904) as the most popular opera written in the twentieth century. The perennially hardy *Butterfly* struggled for life in her first few years; an unfavorable first-night reception in Milan pushed Puccini to reshape the work for what became an enthusiastically greeted production the following spring in Brescia (where the structure of the opera was shifted from two acts to three) with additional fine tunings added for the geisha's arrival in London (1905) and Paris (1906).

Madama Butterfly was taken from a hit play by producer-director David Belasco (itself drawn from a story by John Luther Long), which Puccini had seen in its London run at the Duke of York's Theatre. Despite his almost total lack of fluency in English, Puccini immediately realized the heartstring-twanging potential of Belasco's fifteen-year-old Japanese girl maneuvered into marriage and then abandoned by a callow American naval lieutenant. The reformation of his opera from fiasco to crowd-pleaser was the type of challenge upon which Puccini thrived. Notorious for fussing over his libretti (and his own music) in even the best of times, Puccini played the high-stakes game of making *Butterfly* a success with the editorial ruthlessness that made him the scourge of his collaborators.

Almost all of Puccini's post-Milan revisions for *Madama Butterfly* involved tightening the drama's focus on the central character of Cio-Cio-San (nicknamed Butterfly) and the Eastern code of ethics that makes her choose death over dishonor. In its first operatic incarnation, more was made of Lieutenant Pinkerton's "ugly American" qualities; by the time the opera arrived in Paris, the young officer's rough edges had been smoothed, his anti-Japanese slurs excised, and his last act scene humanized by the addition of a short aria to indicate his remorse. This taming of Pinkerton made him a more effective foil for Butterfly, his softness of temper making her inner steel shine all the more brightly.

Madama Butterfly is the closest thing Puccini ever wrote to a star vehicle. Cio-Cio-San is a role which can make careers and wreck voices. She rarely leaves the stage, driving forward at rapid speed through an emotional minefield of virginal exaltation, sexual ecstasy, mother love, and suicidal despair. A soprano needs to husband her resources of voice and temperament with caution lest she be overwhelmed by Butterfly's shattered heart along with her audience.

After *Butterfly,* Puccini's operas were variously set in California (*La Fanciulla del West*, 1910), the Riviera (*La Rondine*, 1917), and a combination of Parisian barge, Tuscan convent, and Renaissance bedchamber (the three-opera *Il Trittico*, 1918) before returning to an Oriental landscape for his final opera *Turandot* (1926), an ear-filling pageant of ancient Beijing. Puccini succumbed to cancer before he could finish *Turandot*, which was completed for him by the distinguished musician Franco Alfano. At the *Turandot* premiere, seventeen months after Puccini's death, conductor Arturo Toscanini paid a final tribute to the composer by putting down his baton and ending the performance at the page in the score where Puccini's own work had ended.

Madama Butterfly
The child Butterfly is transformed by grief into a woman of dignity.

Madama Butterfly

Opera in 3 Acts

by

Giacomo Puccini

PAGLIACCI

Opera in 2 Acts

by

RUGGERO LEONCAVALLO

(1857–1919)

Libretto: RUGGERO LEONCAVALLO
Premiere: MILAN, TEATRO DAL VERME; MAY 21, 1892

Verismo opera, which walloped the stuffing out of the Italian lyric theatre in the 1890s, presented life on stage in thick, raw slices. The brief but potent vogue for verismo was established in 1890, when publisher Edoardo Sonzogno's contest for the best new one-act opera was won by *Cavalleria Rusticana*, Pietro Mascagni's ferocious Easter Sunday drama of love spurned. The opera swept Italy and was produced in Berlin, Philadelphia, London, and Paris within two years. Mascagni was never able to repeat the success of *Cavalleria*, but its continued importance in the repertory throughout his life maintained his own reputation as a composer and conductor. An unwise alliance with the Fascist regime of Benito Mussolini brought a disgraced old age to the maestro, who died in Rome a few months after VE Day.

Another entrant in Sonzogno's competition was *Pagliacci*, a short tragedy concerning a troupe of itinerant players in Calabria by Ruggero Leoncavallo, a struggling composer dissatisfied with his current publisher. Even though *Pagliacci*'s two-act structure disqualified it for consideration from the contest, Sonzogno accepted it for publication and produced it (1892) at the Teatro del Verme in Milan under the direction of Arturo Toscanini. It also enjoyed immediate popularity, adding the highly charged Canio to the world's repertory of important tenor roles.

Pagliacci begins with a Prologue sung by the clown Tonio, who tells the audience that they are about to see a real story. (The son of a police magistrate, Leoncavallo averred that the plot was taken from one of his father's cases.) When Nedda, wife of the aging player Canio, cuckolds him with the villager Silvio, Canio's mind breaks with strain. During the evening's performance Canio is unable to separate his own situation from that of Pagliacco, the *commedia dell'arte* character he plays, and as the horrified audience watches, the actor stabs his wife and her lover before we hear one of opera's most famous curtain lines: "La commedia è finita! [The comedy is over!]" (Written to be spoken by the baritone Tonio, the line is frequently co-opted by star tenors, who are happiest when they can have the last word.)

In the early years of this century, the role of Canio belonged to the unrivalled tenor Enrico Caruso, who sang more than 100 performances of *Pagliacci* with the Metropolitan Opera Company. Caruso's rise to fame parallelled the development of the phonograph, and it was his recording of Canio's dressing-table lament that made "Vesti la giubba" a hit tune. Identification of role with artist was further strengthened by Herman Mishkin's widely reproduced photographs of the ebullient Neopolitan beating a drum in his capacious white clown costume and pointed hat.

Leoncavallo's later works failed to establish themselves with the electric charge of *Pagliacci*. His own version of *La Bohème* (1897) was soon eclipsed by that of Puccini, and the sharply crafted *Zazà* (1900), once a prima donna favorite, faded from view soon after the composer's death in 1919. *Pagliacci* is most often heard today as half of a double bill with Mascagni's *Cavalleria*, a pairing which has forever united the hot-blooded twins of verismo as *Cav/Pag*.

Above:
Cavalleria Rusticana (1890)
Pietro Mascagni (1863–1945)

Opposite:
Pagliacci
Canio watches the shame of his broken marriage unfold on stage.

Pagliacci

Opera in 2 Acts
by
RUGGERO LEONCAVALLO

THE QUEEN OF SPADES
(PIKOVAYA DAMA)
Opera in 3 Acts
by
PYOTR ILYICH TCHAIKOVSKY
(1840–1893)

Libretto: MODEST TCHAIKOVSKY, AFTER ALEKSANDR PUSHKIN'S STORY
Premiere: ST. PETERSBURG, MARYINSKY TEATR; DECEMBER 19, 1890

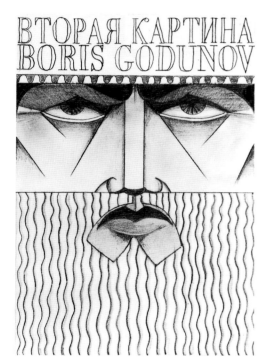

Opera did not arrive in Russia until the eighteenth century, when Italian troupes performed there at the invitation of the royal family. Catherine the Great, a fervent believer in opera's usefulness as social commentary, wrote several opera librettos in her spare hours away from empire management; among her collaborators was the Spaniard Vicente Martín y Soler, the *opera buffa* master admired by Mozart and Da Ponte.

Indigenous Russian opera hit its stride with the works of Mikhail Glinka, whose historical epic *A Life for the Tsar* (1836) and fantasy *Ruslan and Lyudmila* (1842) each combined the muscular oriental power of Russian folk music with the more refined lyric conventions of Western Europe. Modest Mussorgsky, considered by many to be the supreme genius of Russian music, completed only one opera, the massive *Boris Godunov*, before his death in 1881. Alcoholic and undisciplined, Mussorgsky painted an unconventional musical canvas centered on one of opera's greatest bass roles, the guilt-ridden Tsar Boris.

Although Pyotr Tchaikovsky's operas are not as universally beloved as his immortal ballet scores, every balletomane knows at least one Tchaikovsky opera melody: the familiar Act II adagio from *Swan Lake* is "borrowed" from a love duet in the composer's own unproduced opera *Undine*. Material by the Russian poet Aleksandr Pushkin inspired three of Tchaikovsky's greatest successes as an opera composer: *Eugene Onegin* (1879), *Mazeppa* (1884), and *The Queen of Spades* (1890). The latter—Pushkin's ghoulish short story, first published in 1834—is set in the Russia of the Great Catherine. The officer Gherman (Hermann) learns that the elderly Countess Anna Feodorovna possesses a secret formula for winning at faro, a card game. When the overwrought Gherman demands that the old woman give him the formula, she dies of fright. Gherman thinks that the Countess's secret has perished with her until the spectre of the dead woman appears to him and reveals the winning sequence: three, seven, ace. When Gherman next gambles, he bets all he owns on the magic formula but is ruined when the cards turn up as . . . three . . . seven . . . Queen of Spades.

Tchaikovsky's emphasis on the dark side of fate and his own natural melancholy re-ordered the ironic conclusion of Pushkin's story into bleak tragedy. Pushkin's Gherman, shocked into insanity by his loss, is committed to an asylum; Tchaikovsky's protagonist commits suicide at the gambling table. Pushkin also tells us that Lisa, the object of Gherman's romantic attentions, follows her unhappy flirtation with the gambler by marrying "an amiable young man"; the operatic Lisa drowns herself in the waters of the Neva (saving time for a magnificent aria before she jumps, of course).

In the years when few international singers counted Russian fluency in their arsenal of performance skills, it was customary to present *The Queen of Spades* (and most other Russian operas) in translation. The recent parting of the Iron Curtain has introduced more Russian works and Russian singers to the opera houses of the West, making performances of Tchaikovsky's *Queen* in its original language more frequent in the United States and in Europe.

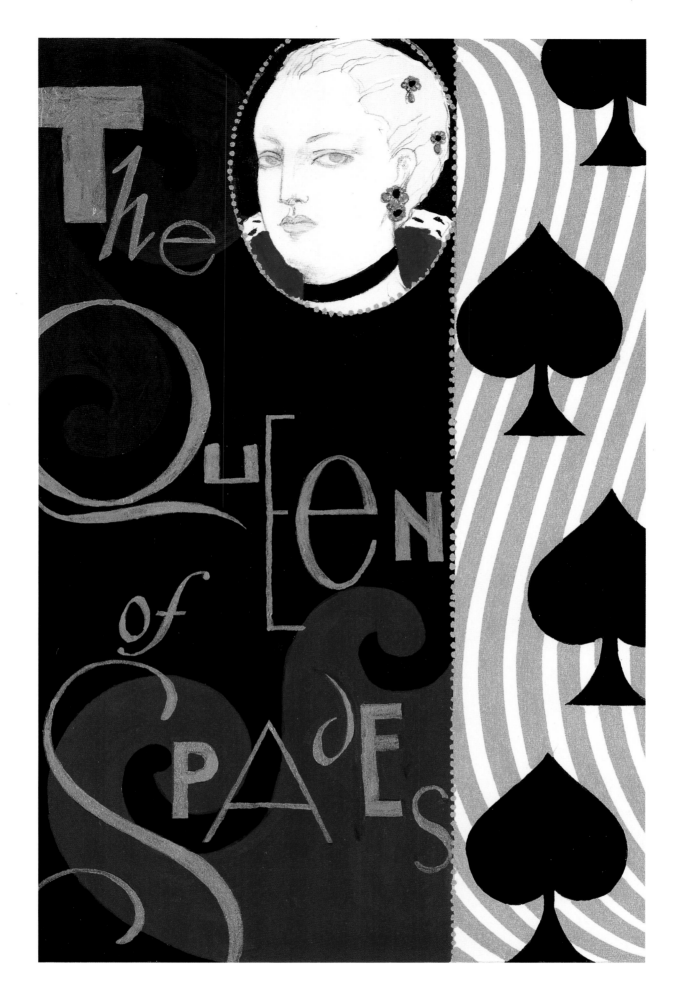

THE QUEEN OF SPADES

Opera in 3 Acts

by

PYOTR ILYICH TCHAIKOVSKY

Faust
Opera in 5 Acts
by
Charles François Gounod
(1818–1893)

Libretto: Jules Barbier and Michel Carré,
after Johann Wolfgang von Goethe's dramatic poem
Premiere: Paris, Théâtre Lyrique; March 19, 1859

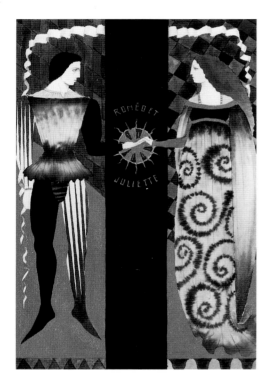

When the Devil offers the elderly scholar Faust a choice of gold, glory, or power, he asks instead for a treasure which he says contains everything: youth. The Devil's price for granting the old man's wish? His immortal soul. As long as Faust remains in this life, the Devil will be at his service; afterward, death will bring an eternity in hell. The scholar accepts the Devil's offer, and the consequences of the bargain have engaged countless playwrights, poets, and opera composers since the sixteenth century, when the legend of Faust and his temptation by Méphistophélès was first published.

Johann Wolfgang von Goethe's dramatic poem *Faust*, issued in two parts in 1808 and 1832, has inspired more than a score of operas, none more successful than the version by Charles Gounod. First heard at the Théâtre Lyrique in 1859, Gounod's *Faust* racked up more than two thousand performances in Paris in the next eighty years despite the inconvenient interruptions of the Franco-Prussian War and World War I. *Faust* was an established United States favorite of twenty years' standing when it was chosen as the inaugural opera (1883) for the Metropolitan Opera House, where it was scheduled so frequently that the exasperated critic W. J. Henderson rechristened the Met the "Faustspielhaus." A perennial favorite at Covent Garden for three generations, *Faust* was also a staple in the repertories of continental European houses. In Germany, where many felt that Gounod made too severe an abridgement of their national poet's greatest work, the opera was performed everywhere but sternly rechristened as *Margarethe* (after the girl Faust woos, impregnates, and abandons).

The seven deadly sins are genrously represented in Gounod's cast of perdition-bound revelers: the callow seducer Faust, the giddy, easily tempted Marguerite and her bellicose brother Valentin, the lusty widow Marthe and the querulous youth Siebel, all dominated by Méphistophélès, a witty, magnetic roué of undeniable (if devilish) charm. A refined yet optimistic buoyancy marks the entire score, from the infectiously pulsing waltz in the kermesse scene to the sparkling filigree of Marguerite's famous "jewel song" and the hair-raising Soldier's Chorus, "Gloire immortelle de nos aieux." Gounod's religious sincerity and melodic elan build the drama to a colossal climax in the final scene as the imprisoned Marguerite, condemned to death for murdering her newborn child, calls on God for redemption. When Faust begs Marguerite to escape with him, the overwhelmed girl cries out that his hands are stained with blood and falls dead at his feet. Marguerite's soul is called to grace by a heavenly choir and Faust is dragged down to hell by Méphistophélès.

In *Roméo et Juliette*, Gounod's condensation of Shakespeare's tragedy, the progression of the love story hews fairly close to the original save that the necessity of a final duet prevents Roméo from preceding Juliette in death by any great distance. The opera betrays its nineteenth-century origins most clearly in the characterization of Juliette, who is no impulsive Italian girl new to love but a gracious, self-possessed prima donna, the phrases of her first waltz song snapping open with the sharpness of a jeweled fan.

Above:
Roméo et Juliette (1867)

Opposite:
Faust
The philosopher examines heaven and earth to find the meaning of life.

Faust

Opera in 5 Acts
by

CHARLES FRANÇOIS GOUNOD

CARMEN
Opera in 4 Acts
by
GEORGES BIZET
(1838–1875)

Libretto: HENRI MEILHAC AND LUDOVIC HALÉVY, AFTER PROSPER MÉRIMÉE'S NOVEL
Premiere: PARIS, OPÉRA-COMIQUE; MARCH 3, 1875

One of the world's most popular operas started life as a colossal flop. Today, in the light of its present classic status, the initial failure of *Carmen* seems impossible, but the unbridled passion of Bizet's gypsy girl roundly offended the notoriously stuffy Parisian bourgeoisie of 1875. The sophisticated Viennese were the first to embrace *Carmen* when a successful German-language production was mounted in the autumn following the Paris premiere. Within three years, Mademoiselle had travelled successfully to London and New York and her appeal was soon universally recognized. *Carmen*, acclaimed as Georges Bizet's masterpiece, was his last work for the theatre; three months after its dismal first night, he died at the age of thirty-six.

None of Bizet's previous operas approach the quality of *Carmen*. The sentimental Scots romance *La Jolie fille de Perth* (1867) contains Bizet's most unusual heroine, Catherine Glover, who is cured of temporary madness by a tenor serenade. *Les Pêcheurs de perles* (1863), set on the island of Ceylon, and the Cairo-bound *Djamileh* (1872) reflect the French nineteenth-century fashion for exotic locales and use liberal doses of musical orientalisms to disguise preposterous story lines. The libretto for *Carmen* is easily the best ever set by Bizet, containing many striking (and often violent) dramatic situations for his musical gifts. Originally written as an *opéra comique* with its musical sections connected by spoken dialogue, *Carmen* was posthumously fitted with sung recitatives that gave the piece a Grand Opera atmosphere Bizet never intended. Most modern productions return the opera to the more spontaneous sound of its original format.

Who is Carmen? A gypsy girl employed in a Seville cigarette factory, Carmen is a lithe, physically fearless beauty who drives men berserk. She knows what (or who) she wants and gets it (or him) with no apologies or regrets. Her only important possession is her freedom, and it is as a free woman that Carmen meets death, unfettered by love or fear as she is stabbed by an ex-admirer.

Carmen is as tempting to prima donnas as she is to the gentlemen of Seville. Her music is irresistible, with two knockout arias, the "Habanera" and the "Seguidilla," packed into the first act alone. She brawls, dances, plays the castanets, reads fortunes, snags herself a tenor and a baritone, and caps the evening with a splendid death scene. A warning to budding divas: the list of artists who have sung Carmen is quite long but the number of truly successful Carmens is rather small. Only a brave and honest singer belongs in this role; faux Carmens are swiftly betrayed by their clichéd gestures. Once a hands-on-hips stance was the standard-issue pose; nowadays a combination of bare feet, bad posture, and truculent lips seems to be the equally tiresome vogue. Carmen will survive these trifling indignities, choosing, as always, to ignore any spirit less free than her own.

Carmen
Carmen's boldness and strength are irresistible.

Carmen

Opera in 4 Acts
by
GEORGES BIZET

CENDRILLON
(CINDERELLA)
Conte de Fées in 4 Acts & 6 Tableaux
by
JULES MASSENET
(1842–1912)

Libretto: HENRI CAIN, AFTER CHARLES PERRAULT'S STORY
Premiere: PARIS, OPÉRA-COMIQUE; MAY 24, 1899

If you are suffering neglect but happen to be young and beautiful, take heart: relief will be arriving shortly in the person of a handsome prince. So we are told in the classic fairy tale of Cinderella, which has existed in the world's folk literature for a thousand years. Scholars of mythology see the immutably hopeful Cinderella as a symbol of the dawn, pursued by the night clouds of disagreeable relations until she is rescued by the benevolent sun.

The little drudge turned princess achieved her most familiar incarnation in critic Charles Perrault's *Histoires ou contes du temps passé* (1697), the setting of the story that established Cinderella as a distinctly French heroine. Who but a Frenchwoman could achieve so much with a simple change of wardrobe? (Her natural chic notwithstanding, Cinderella's boldest ballroom fashion statement was inadvertently designed by an English translator who misread Perrault's phrase *pantoufles en vair* [slippers of fur] as *pantoufles en verre* [of glass], a more picturesque but equally impractical material for dancing shoes.)

The girl with the midnight curfew had been the subject of several operas before Jules Massenet's *Cendrillon*. In the most famous of these, Rossini's *La Cenerentola* (1817), she is a big-hearted, generous comedienne, redolent of warm Italian sunshine. Massenet's French Cinderella is a fey, gentle creature given to wistful soliloquies in the moonlight. She is dreamy enough to be called somnolent, sleeping soundly through the deliciously scored entrance of her Fairy Godmother and the gang of elfin couturiers who awaken her when it is ball time. In order to establish a celestial, otherworldly communion between Cendrillon and her lover, Massenet wrote Le Prince Charmant for soprano, leaving strict instructions that the lady engaged for the role have a *physique* appropriate for breeches. When Le Prince and Cendrillon pledge eternal love in a shared nocturnal episode of bewitched slumber, the young boy shows his sensitivity by hanging his own broken, bleeding heart in the branches of a magic oak tree. Cendrillon considerately returns this macabre token of affection in the opera's final levee scene.

Jules Massenet rarely challenged his audiences but always charmed them. It was with *Manon* (1884), the tale of a country girl turned courtesan, that he was established as the leading French composer of his day; for the rest of his life Massenet would be able to live handsomely off his opera royalties as success followed success. Dismissed by his critics as a mere *pâtissier,* a composer of pretty confections who pandered to popular taste, Massenet had an undeniable affinity for the sympathetic musical portraiture of the woman fallen (or in mid-fall), be it in *ancien régime* France (*Manon*), fourth century Egypt (*Thaïs,* 1894), or modern Paris (*Sapho,* 1897).

As the nineteenth century ended in France (a process which took longer there than in the rest of the world) and modernism became the mode, Massenet's reputation went into an unduly precipitous decline. Despite renewed appreciation of the composer's dramatic gifts, only his *Manon* and *Werther* (1892) enjoy current favor, and the enchanting *Cendrillon* now sleeps again.

Cendrillon
Every step Cinderella takes brings her closer to midnight.

Cendrillon

Conte de Fées in 4 Acts & 6 Tableaux
by

JULES MASSENET

PELLÉAS ET MÉLISANDE
Opéra in 5 Acts
by
CLAUDE DEBUSSY
(1862–1918)

Libretto: MAURICE MAETERLINCK
Premiere: PARIS, OPÉRA-COMIQUE; APRIL 30, 1902

Pelléas et Mélisande is the only completed opera by Claude Debussy, the French musician celebrated for his exquisite piano compositions and sumptuously colored works for orchestra. Debussy spent a decade on the composition of *Pelléas*, spinning its diaphanous musical texture with exacting patience and shaping the singers' vocal lines with the inflections and rhythms of an intimate conversation.

The opera began life as a play by the Belgian dramatist Maurice Maeterlinck, a leading figure in the Symbolist movement of the late nineteenth century. The Symbolists adored fairy tales, in which the seemingly simple interaction of mythic characters evoked the more complex desires and emotions of the contemporary European maelstrom; the landscape of the subconscious was their favorite *mise en scène*.

The plot is ingeniously artless. Mélisande arrives in medieval Allemonde as the bride of old King Arkel's grandson Golaud. When Golaud's half-brother Pelléas and Mélisande fall in love, the enraged Golaud kills Pelléas. Heartbroken, Mélisande dies in childbirth. It is the unique synergy of Maeterlinck's wounded characters and Debussy's shimmering musical setting that extends the action beyond its fairy-tale setting into the dimension of unspoken yearning, loss, and pain.

When *Pelléas et Mélisande* was first produced as a play, sophisticated theatre-goers—those unflinching pillars of the avant-garde—accepted its adolescent heroine as a creature of elemental mystery whose frequent silences and elliptical turns of phrase marked a strength of purpose as potent as the outspoken, swaggering theatricality of the "new women" celebrated by Shaw, Pinero, and Ibsen. For a few decades after her fin de siècle birth date, the secretive Mélisande lost ground in the pantheon of the twentieth century's more self-aggrandizing lyric heroines. Mélisande's inscrutability has become less troublesome in today's world, where the most complicated psychological problems are routinely reduced to pop-culture jargon. The girl-next-door is now a passive-aggressive, and Mélisande, once a timeless enigma, is a woman of the new millennium.

Pelléas et Mélisande
A farewell meeting holds a confession of love.

Pelléas et Mélisande

Opera in 5 Acts
by
Claude Debussy

ELEKTRA
Opera in 1 Act
by
RICHARD STRAUSS
(1864–1949)

Libretto: HUGO VON HOFMANNSTHAL, AFTER SOPHOCLES'S TRAGEDY
Premiere: DRESDEN, KÖNIGLICHES OPERNHAUS; JANUARY 25, 1909

Above:
Salome (1905)

Opposite:
Elektra
Elektra shouts for the gods to avenge
her father's murder.

The operatic career of Richard Strauss is proof that time and success can transform even the most committed radical into a reactionary. Once vilified as shockingly unconventional, Strauss's operas acquired the comforting patina of nostalgia long before the end of his career. The composer established his early reputation with a series of ornately emotional symphonic poems and by the 1905 premiere of *Salome*, his first great operatic success, had pushed the lush romanticism of the nineteenth century into an almost savage garishness. The libretto, taken from Oscar Wilde's play, shaped the story of John the Baptist and Herod's light-footed stepdaughter—sufficiently unpleasant for most people as reported for posterity by Sts. Matthew and Mark—into a lavishly detailed study of turpitude. Every scrap of fetishism, incest, and necrophilia present at the court of the Galilean tetrarch is magnified by Strauss's neurotically sensual score. Many operagoers were revolted by *Salome*'s frank eroticism; in 1907, the puritannical blue bloods of the Metropolitan Opera House's Golden Horseshoe banned the opera after a single performance. The once outrageous *Salome* has now been writhing her way through opera houses all over the world for almost a century, but her audaciousness still bears the bloom of youth; season after season, no other opera lends itself quite so well to the depiction of vigorous, auditorium-filling decadence.

Richard Strauss's greatest works for the opera were written in collaboration with the Austrian poet and librettist Hugo von Hofmannsthal. The two men were vastly different in temperament and artistic taste but worked together well—perhaps because most of their professional discussions were conducted by mail. *Elektra*, their first teaming, is adapted from Sophocles' tragedy of the Mycenaen princess and makes matters *chez Herod* look almost tame by comparison. Salome makes herself crazy in the course of her opera; Elektra begins her opera crazed with grief and then proceeds to drive everyone else in her family mad as well. Disfunctional families had appeared in opera before the advent of *Elektra*, but never had been exhibited or pilloried with quite the same enthusiasm that Strauss and von Hofmannsthal brought to the task.

The ghoulish conversation between Elektra and the anxiety-ridden queen Klytämnestra is surely unique in the annals of heart-to-heart mother and daughter chats. When Klytämnestra complains piteously of sleeplessness and nightmares, Elektra advises impassively that sleep will come if a sacrifice is made. "A virgin bride or a woman knowledgeable about men?" asks the queen. "*Knowledgeable*. That's it," shoots back Elektra, her eyes gleaming with thoughts of matricide. The guilty parties in this opera are all dispatched offstage, the better to leave the courtyard of the palace clear for Elektra's final dance of triumph.

ELEKTRA

Opera in 1 Act

by

RICHARD STRAUSS

DER ROSENKAVALIER

Opera in 3 Acts

by

RICHARD STRAUSS
(1864–1949)

Libretto: HUGO VON HOFMANNSTHAL
Premiere: DRESDEN, KÖNIGLICHES OPERNHAUS; JANUARY 26, 1911

Der Rosenkavalier, the glittering comedy of manners which typifies Richard Strauss's mature style, is an altogether cozier affair than either of his two earlier family dramas. Hearts are broken—this is opera, after all—but nobody dies, not even off stage. *Der Rosenkavalier* is an operatic paradox: a twentieth-century work set in the rococo splendor of eighteenth-century Vienna that moves in waltz time, a nineteenth-century musical signature. The plot is a classic love quadrangle, in which a chic older woman watches her toothsome young lover leave her to rescue a guileless girl from an unsuitable marriage to a boorish aristocrat. The characters are gallantly sentimental—there is much smiling through tears—and the music courses through three elegantly crafted acts in an irresistibly seductive rhythm.

    Der Rosenkavalier has three of Strauss's greatest soprano roles: the convent-bred ingénue Sophie, the soignée but warmhearted Marschallin, and the impetuous Octavian, Count Rofrano, whose bearing of a silver rose in a Viennese courtship ceremony gives the opera its name. The Count dominates the opera as written but with the passage of time the introspective Marschallin has moved to center stage. Octavian is young, wealthy, and good-looking, a triple-bonus condition that few of us have experienced first hand. The Marschallin, on the other hand, is trying to grow older with as much grace as she can muster—a plan of action that inspires empathy in all of us. The fashion in Marschallins has grown increasingly mature; as the lady sings beautiful music in the first and third acts and has a nice long rest in-between, the role is one in which prima donnas can grow comfortably old. The Marschallin, however, is supposed to be only thirty-two. To play the lady well into her sixties, as some divas have, transforms boudoir passion into somewhat skittish maternalism. The Marschallin's love affair with Octavian should not be a farewell performance but rather the latest in a sequence of cleverly managed extra-curricular dalliances that have marked her married life. Madame seems bereft at the story's end, but her heart is of the variety which heals swiftly when broken. All of what we have just seen—the laughter, the tears, the well-practiced aristocratic resignation—has probably happened before. It could very easily happen again, couldn't it?

Der Rosenkavalier
A silver rose carries the perfume of love in rococo Vienna.

Der Rosenkavalier

Opera in 3 Acts

by

RICHARD STRAUSS

Top:
Die Frau ohne Schatten (1919)

Above:
Daphne (1938)

Opposite:
Ariadne auf Naxos
Notions of love are transposed when
Ariadne and Zerbinetta meet on the
isle of Naxos.

ARIADNE AUF NAXOS
Opera in 1 Act & a Scenic Prelude
by
RICHARD STRAUSS
(1864–1949)

Libretto: HUGO VON HOFMANNSTHAL
Premiere: STUTTGART; OCTOBER 25, 1912
Premiere: revised version: VIENNA, COURT OPERA; OCTOBER 4, 1916

Ariadne auf Naxos, which went through a massive revision before von Hofmannsthal and Strauss felt they got it right, is another soprano-rich comedy. *Ariadne's* featured trouser role is the distraught, headstrong young Composer who spars with a termagant Prima Donna in a gossipy backstage plot that combines one-liners, musical advice, and Greek tragedy. (Revised operas often have confusing plots, and *Ariadne* is no exception.)

The third soprano role in *Ariadne* is the comedienne Zerbinetta, who is assigned a coloratura aria so difficult and so long that it resembles a circus act with high notes. On and on and on she sings, with trills, cadenzas, and spiraling runs packed into every page of the score. Few singers who attempt Zerbinetta emerge unscathed; like trapeze artists, Zerbinettas must either succeed completely or plunge to their deaths with everyone watching. When a good Zerbinetta takes a bow, she is greeted with cheers worthy of a matador who has just dispatched a particularly trouble-some bull. As well she should be, for in Ariadne the specter of the Minotaur is never very far away.

Richard Strauss adored the soprano voice and exploited its musical expressive-ness with long, soaring vocal lines that float like gossamer over his massive orchestral texture. Moravian soprano Maria Jeritza, who created roles in *Ariadne auf Naxos* and the phantasmagoric *Die Frau ohne Schatten* (1919), said that, "He makes [musical] phrases which go from here to Brook-e-lyn! They make me *choke*." The ultimate Richard Strauss soprano aria is probably the final scene from *Daphne* (1938), in which a nymph is transmuted into a laurel tree by Zeus. Daphne's vocal line breasts the crashing orchestra, rising in intensity and fervor as she gains release into immor-tality. Violins, harps, and winds surround her and then her voice disappears; a brief orchestral interlude follows and dissolves into the barest of string accompaniment. Then Daphne's disembodied voice returns, a whispered echo in the wind. It is Strauss, not Zeus, who makes us hear the girl sprout branches and leaves.

Strauss's favorite soprano had to be his wife, the monumentally difficult Pauline de Ahna, who created Freihild in his early opera *Guntram* (1894). They met when Strauss was conducting at the Mannheim Opera. When Strauss corrected her singing in a rehearsal, de Ahna threw the score at him. She missed his head but struck his heart, for he fell in love with her instantly. Something of a domestic tyrant as Frau Strauss, Pauline forbid household visitors to wear shoes lest they spoil her expensive carpets and constantly nagged Strauss to compose more. Strauss's 1924 opera *Intermezzo,* the story of a celebrity marriage almost wrecked by a misdelivered love letter, was suggested by an incident in his life with the trying but much-beloved Pauline.

A RIADNE auf N AXOS

Opera in 1 Act & a Scenic Prelude

by

RICHARD STRAUSS

BILLY BUDD

Opera in 4 Acts

by

BENJAMIN BRITTEN

(1913–1976)

Libretto: E. M. FORSTER AND ERIC CROZIER, AFTER HERMAN MELVILLE'S NOVEL
Premiere: LONDON, COVENT GARDEN; DECEMBER 1, 1951

While London has always been one of the world's great operatic capitals, opera in England remained a largely foreign-born affair until the advent of Benjamin Britten. The short career of Henry Purcell yielded the eternally poignant *Dido and Aeneas* (1689), but few other subsequent English works hold the stage in the modern repertory save for the canon born of William Schwenk Gilbert and Arthur Sullivan's felicitous partnership (1875–1896).

With the 1945 premiere of *Peter Grimes*, a tale taken from George Crabbe's poem *The Village*, Britten and his embittered, lonely Suffolk fisherman brought English opera international recognition; success at Sadler's Wells was followed by productions throughout Europe and the United States. A series of chamber operas engaged Britten until the opening of his next full-scale theatrical work, *Billy Budd*.

Herman Melville's story of an innocent merchant sailor sacrificed to preserve a military code of discipline resonated powerfully in the post–World War II age; an Italian operatic setting by Giorgio Ghedini was given in Venice in 1949, and a Broadway adaptation of the book was a critical success in the same year that Britten's opera opened. Billy's Christ-like purity of spirit isolates him from the hostile world of the man o' war *Indomitable* and reflects a central theme in much of Britten's work: the individual crushed by the intolerance of society. The English tenor Peter Pears, Britten's companion for most of his adult life, was *Billy Budd*'s first Captain Vere. It was Britten's unique understanding of Pears's interpretative gifts that gave us the tortured Grimes; the Earl of Essex, arrogant lover of *Gloriana* (1953); *The Turn of the Screw*'s unspeakable ghoul Quint (1954); and the doomed Aschenbach in *Death in Venice* (1973), their last collaboration before Britten's death.

The polar opposite of the preternaturally valorous Billy Budd is the amoral centerpiece of Alban Berg's opera *Lulu*, who begins her career as a bride and ends it as a prostitute. Lulu showers bad luck on her amours, who are dispatched by heart attack, razor, gunshot and neglect, before meeting her own crimson-edged demise at the hands of Jack the Ripper. Left unfinished at Berg's death in 1935, *Lulu* was given its first (incomplete) mounting in Zurich two years later; a German production had been opposed by the Nazis, who deemed Berg's music insufficiently Aryan in spirit. As Berg's widow refused to release any unpublished or unorchestrated material relating to the opera, it was not until after her death in 1976 that a completed version of *Lulu* was published. The Paris Opéra's 1979 production at last brought *Lulu* to life in all her careless, flippant wickedness.

Above:
Lulu (1937; 1979)
Alban Berg (1885–1935)

Opposite:
Billy Budd
Foretopman Billy Budd serves on
the man o' war HMS *Indomitable*.

Billy Budd

Opera in 4 Acts

by

BENJAMIN BRITTEN

The Ballad of Baby Doe

Opera in 2 Acts

by

Douglas Moore

(1893–1969)

Libretto: John Latouche
Premiere: Central City, Colorado; July 7, 1956

Douglas Moore's *The Ballad of Baby Doe* is based on an American tabloid love story. In 1880, silver magnate Horace Tabor scandalized the state of Colorado by leaving his rock-ribbed wife, Augusta, for the plump, pretty embrace of Mrs. Elizabeth ("Baby") Doe. Horace and Baby eventually married, but the stigma of their adulterous relationship excluded the couple from polite society in Denver despite their storied buying power. When Horace lost his fortune, Baby stuck by him, even after death; in 1935, she was found frozen to death in her cabin at the Matchless Mine, source of much of Horace's wealth.

The world premiere of *Baby Doe* in Central City, Colorado, was such a success that there was talk of a transfer to Broadway; the prospective backers eventually withdrew, allowing the New York City Opera to present its own production as part of a month-long all-American season in the spring of 1958. Walter Cassel (Horace) and Martha Lipton (Augusta) were veterans of the Central City production; the superlative new Baby Doe was Beverly Sills, who made the haunting "Letter Scene" and "Silver Song" her own.

Original American opera has been produced in a variety of venues. In 1910, the Metropolitan Opera House presented its first American opera, *The Pipe of Desire,* the tale of an Elf King by Frederick Shepherd Converse, a Boston composer. American operas subsequently premiered at the Old Met were Horatio Parker's *Mona* (1912), Deems Taylor's *Peter Ibbetson* (1931), Louis Gruenberg's *The Emperor Jones* (1933), and Gian Carlo Menotti's *The Island God* (1942). Douglas Moore's own one-act opera *The Devil and Daniel Webster* (1939) bowed in a Broadway production, as did Kurt Weill's *Street Scene* (1947), Mark Blitzstein's *Regina* (1949), adapted from Lillian Hellman's *The Little Foxes,* and Leonard Bernstein's *Candide* (1956). Virgil Thomson's regally witty *Four Saints in Three Acts* (1934) and Carlisle Floyd's folk-flavored *Susannah* (1955) were both first heard in regional theatres, as was Scott Joplin's joyous ragtime opera *Treemonisha* (composed 1907–1911, premiered 1972).

Treemonisha is the tale of a charismatic foundling girl discovered in the shade of a tree near an Arkansas plantation cabin. Her education makes her a powerful force for good in her small African-American community, mirroring the strong pro-education stance of Joplin himself. The Texas-born son of an ex-slave, Joplin was America's "King of Ragtime," a vaudeville headliner whose catchy piano rags brought him national fame. A strong attraction to the musical theatre never won Joplin much luck there as a composer. His only copy of his opera *The Guest of Honor* (1903) was lost, making his hopes for the success of *Treemonisha* a virtual obsession. Joplin published the opera's piano-vocal score himself in a desperate attempt to promote *Treemonisha,* but the only performance before his death in 1917 was a run-through in a Harlem rehearsal hall. *Treemonisha* finally bowed in a semi-professional production at Atlanta's Morehouse College in 1972, with a presentation by the Houston Grand Opera following three years later.

Above:
Treemonisha (c. 1907)
Scott Joplin (1868–1917)

Opposite:
The Ballad of Baby Doe
A golden-hearted beauty catches both the eye and the fortune of a silver magnate.

The Ballad of Baby Doe

Opera in 2 Acts

by

Douglas Moore

Antony and Cleopatra

Opera in 3 Acts

by

Samuel Barber

(1910–1981)

Libretto: Franco Zeffirelli, after Shakespeare's tragedy
Premiere: New York, Metropolitan Opera House; September 16, 1966

When the Metropolitan Opera moved to a new home in 1966, Samuel Barber was chosen to write the opera for the company's inaugural performance there. The smashing success of Barber's *Vanessa* (1958) in its own world-premiere production at the Old Met made the new commission inevitable for the Pennsylvania-born composer, who considered several subjects (among them the life of Pocahontas) before deciding upon an operatic setting of Shakespeare's *Antony and Cleopatra* to open the Lincoln Center house. The Puerto Rican bass Justino Díaz was cast as Antony opposite the Cleopatra of American soprano Leontyne Price, a Juilliard-trained soprano with a distinguished association with Barber, his music, and the Metropolitan Opera.

The first night of the new opera was front-page news all over the world. The eagerly-awaited conjunction of Price, Barber, and the Serpent of the Nile provided moments of undeniable glory but the premiere of *Antony and Cleopatra* was accounted a disappointment. Music, drama, and the stage machinery itself were overwhelmed by Franco Zeffirelli's lavish production, and aside from two of Cleopatra's incandescent monologues (later expanded into independent concert scenes), the score was long neglected.

It is here that we must remind ourselves that operatic failure is often a temporary condition. *Carmen* and *Madama Butterfly*, now on the short list of the world's most popular operas, were once deemed fiascos by opera critics, while *Faust* and *L'Africaine,* considered to be unshakeable repertory staples early in the twentieth century, find little favor with today's audiences. Perhaps one day *Antony and Cleopatra*—and other works received less than rapturously on first hearing—will win classic status. As revised by Gian Carlo Menotti, the opera has recently been re-evaluated in successful productions by the Spoleto Festival and the Lyric Opera of Chicago.

The Metropolitan Opera's world premieres of the last decade are both highly theatrical works that stretch the conventions of narrative, character, and melody. John Corigliano's *The Ghosts of Versailles* bowed at the Met in 1991 to critical approbation. William Hoffman's libretto, which combined the shades of Marie Antoinette and her courtiers with the characters from the plays of Pierre Beaumarchais, was praised equally with Corigliano's score, an imaginative pastiche of classical and contemporary musical styles. In 1992, the Met celebrated the quadricentennial of Columbus's expedition to the New World with its first opera featuring singing astronauts in Philip Glass and David Henry Hwang's *The Voyage* (1992).

New American Opera seems to be thriving in companies throughout the United States, but the gods, goddesses, and emperors of the Renaissance librettos have been replaced by figures from contemporary mythology. In *Nixon in China* (Houston, 1987), the spare minimalism of composer John Adams and poet-librettist Alice Goodman infused modern newsmakers with archetypal power, earning the piece (and its many successors) the genre sobriquet "CNN Opera."

After more than four centuries, opera remains the ultimate festival art form, happiest when its every performance is presented (and received) as a unique and special occasion. Opera's continuing life is a cause for celebration. When the right balance is struck between words and music, text and performance, singer and song, there is nothing more fantastic.

Antony and Cleopatra
Marc Antony recalls the charms of Cleopatra.

ANTONY AND CLEOPATRA

Opera in 3 Acts

by

SAMUEL BARBER

SELECTED BIBLIOGRAPHY

Christiansen, Rupert. *Prima Donna: A History*. New York: Viking, 1985.

Cross, Milton. *The New Milton Cross' Complete Stories of the Great Operas*. Garden City: Doubleday & Co., Inc.; rev. ed., 1955.

Culshaw, John. *Wagner: The Man and his Music*. The Metropolitan Opera Guild composer series. New York: E. P. Dutton, 1978.

Dizikes, John. *Opera in America: A Cultural History*. New Haven and London: Yale University Press, 1993.

Hamilton, David, ed., and Paul Gruber, exec. ed. *The Metropolitan Opera Encyclopedia: A Comprehensive Guide to the World of Opera*. New York: Simon and Schuster and The Metropolitan Opera Guild, Inc., 1987.

Hume, Paul. *Verdi: The Man and His Music*. The Metropolitan Opera Guild composer series. New York: E. P. Dutton, 1977.

Jackson, Stanley. *Monsieur Butterfly: The Life of Giacomo Puccini*. Briarcliff Manor: Stein and Day, 1974.

Kerman, Joseph. *Opera as Drama*. New York: Alfred A. Knopf, 1956; rev. reprint ed., Berkeley and Los Angeles: University of California Press, 1988.

Radic, Thérèse. *Melba: The Voice of Australia*. S. Melbourne: The Macmillan Company of Australia Pty Ltd., 1986.

Rasponi, Lanfranco. *The Last Prima Donnas*. New York: Alfred A. Knopf, 1982.

Rich, Alan. *The Simon and Schuster Listener's Guide to Opera*. New York: Simon and Schuster, 1980.

Rosand, Ellen. *Opera in Seventeenth Century Venice*. Berkeley and Los Angeles: The University of California Press, 1991.

Sadie, Stanley, ed. *The New Grove Dictionary of Music and Musicians*. London: Macmillan Publishers Limited, 6th ed., 1980.

Scherer, Barrymore Laurence. "Moonlight, Magic and Massenet." CBS Records, 1979.

Scott, Michael. *The Record of Singing*. New York: Charles Scribner's Sons, 1977.

Simon, Henry W. *The Victor Book of the Opera*. New York: Simon and Schuster, 13th ed., 1968.

Sokol, Martin L. *The New York City Opera: An American Adventure*. New York: Macmillan Publishing Co., Inc., 1981.

Stockdale, F. M., and M. R. Dreyer. *The Opera Guide*. London: Collins & Brown, Ltd., 1990.

Tanner, Michael. *Wagner*. Princeton: Princeton University Press, 1996.

Tuggle, Robert. *The Golden Age of Opera*. New York: Holt, Rinehart and Winston, 1983.

Warrack, John, and Ewan West, eds. *The Oxford Dictionary of Opera*. Oxford and New York: Oxford University Press, 1992.

ART DIRECTOR: John Martinez

EDITOR: Ruth A. Peltason
DESIGNER: Darilyn Lowe Carnes

PAGE 2: Detail from *Un Ballo in Maschera* by Giuseppe Verdi (see pages 30–31)

Portions of the sections on Monteverdi and Debussy have appeared in a different form in *Opera News*.

Library of Congress Cataloging-in-Publication Data
Martinez, John.
    Fantastic opera / illustrations by John Martinez ; text by F. Paul Driscoll
        p.   cm.
    Includes bibliographical references.
    ISBN 0–8109–2770–5 (paperback)
    1. Opera—Pictorial works.   2. Opera.   I. Driscoll, F. Paul.
II. Title.
ML1700.M16   1997
782.1—dc21   97–5080

Illustrations copyright © 1997 John Martinez
Text copyright © F. Paul Driscoll

Harry N. Abrams, Inc.
100 Fifth Avenue
New York, N.Y. 10011
www.abramsbooks.com